BIBLIOTHECA HISTORICA CYPRIA

CYPRUS UNDER AN ENGLISH KING

A MAP OF CYPRUS
IN THE TWELFTH CENTURY.

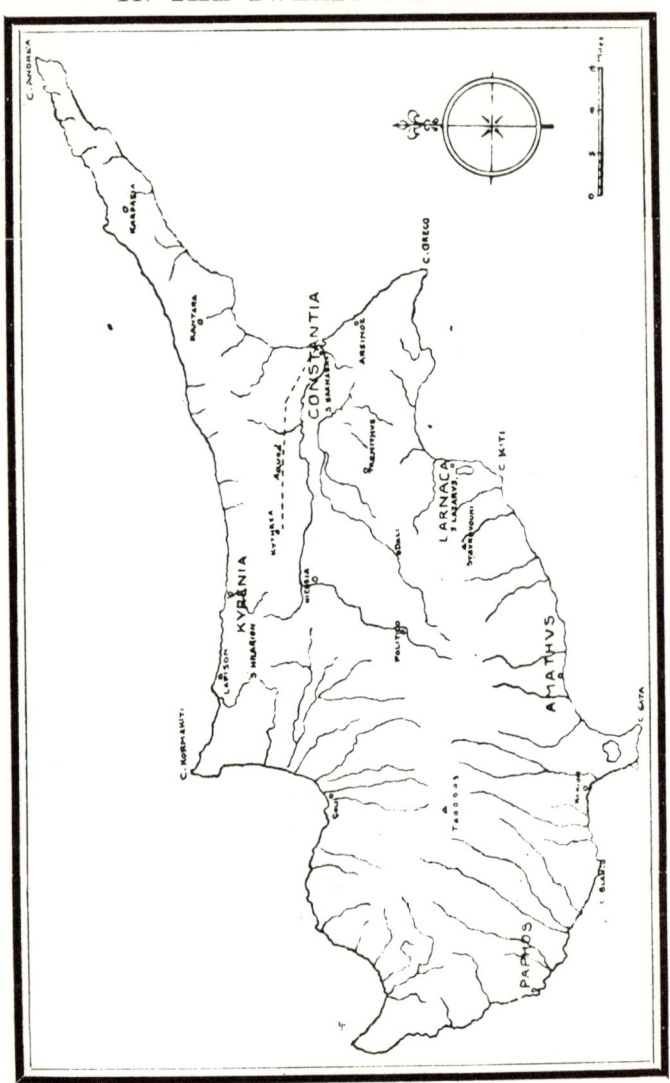

Place names as known to the Crusaders.

CYPRUS

UNDER AN ENGLISH KING

IN THE TWELFTH CENTURY

The adventures of Richard I. and the crowning of his Queen in the island.

BY

GEO. JEFFERY, O.B.E., F.S.A.

ZENO
BOOKSELLERS & PUBLISHERS
LONDON   1973

LIBRARY OF CONGRESS CATALOG No. 72-94765

ISBN 0 900834 77 3

First Published Nicosia 1926
Re-issued London 1973

Zeno Booksellers and Publishers
6, Denmark Street, London WC2H 8LP
England

PREFACE.

IN attempting to paraphrase the ancient chronicles of the Third Crusade, the effort has been to combine the famous diary of the eye-witness Geoffrey de Vinsauf, (Bohn's edition 1849,) the "Itinerarium Regis Anglorum Richardi," with other available sources of information.

Vinsauf (the origin of whose name seems doubtful, but who was probably the Cellarer, or Steward of a Benedictine Monastery), Richard of Devizes, and Roger of Howden (Hoveden), are the chief English chroniclers of the most stirring episode in the history of the Crusades, but there are numerous foreign contemporary records of the greatest importance: the chronicles of Ernoul, William of Tyre, Jacques de Vitry, or the romances of the Fleming "Jean d'Avesnes," or the "Minstrel of Rheims." The foreign sources of information on the adventurous progress of the Third Crusade, whilst giving due prominence to the important figure of Richard Cœur de Lion, as the protagonist of the great epic, are more concerned with the events which took place in the Holy Land than with the incidental occupation of Cyprus by the Anglo-Normans.

In endeavouring to realize the circumstances of the first European occupation of Cyprus, *la Vie Féodale de la Noblesse* of the period must be described in the light of modern research carried on by innumerable students of mediæval history during the past half century : Viollet le Duc, Rey, Schlumberger, and a host of others.

This sketch will fulfil its purpose if it serve as a reminder of those curious and interesting associations which link the beautiful island of Cyprus with England. To Englishmen, the heirs of the Anglo-Normans, such associations of long ago, continued to some extent by the Levant Company of intervening centuries, and now consolidated by the island becoming a regular British Colony, must always be of interest.

I must record my thanks to my wife for the index and to the Government Printer for proof reading and valuable assistance.

G. J.

ILLUSTRATIONS.

	PAGE.
COATS OF ARMS: Normandy and France as used in the third Crusade, Jerusalem from the supposed tomb of King John de Briems, at Assisi	1
FAMILY COATS OF ARMS .. 12, 70, 86 131, 142, 154,	161
ARBALETE A TOUR	36
"MATEGRIFFON"	40
A CROSSBOWMAN	49
VIEW OF AMATHUS	82
A KNIGHT	99
TOMBSTONE, RAOUL DE BLANCHEGARDE	110
TOMBSTONE, UNIDENTIFIED	122
BATTLEFIELD OF TREMYTHUS	125

MAPS.

CYPRUS IN THE TWELFTH CENTURY	*Frontispiece.*
PLAN OF AMATHUS	61
PLAN OF CONSTANTIA	116

CHRONOLOGY OF THE REIGN OF RICHARD I.

A.D.	England.	France.	Events.
1187	Henry II. proposes to join the Crusade.	Philip II. proclaims the Third Crusade.	Guy de Lusignan defeated at Tiberias.
1188	—	—	—
1189	Richard I. joins Crusade.	Crusaders meet Vezelai.	Frederick I. joins Crusade.
1190	Richard I. arrives Messina 23/9.	Philip arrives Messina 16/9.	Crusaders 6 months Messina.
1191	Richard takes Cyprus 7/5.	Philip returns to France 24/12.	Crusaders at Acre.
1192	Richard returns to Europe.	—	Crusade abandoned.
1193	Richard prisoner in Germany.	Philip overruns Normandy.	Guy de Lusignan Lord of Cyprus.
1194	Richard returns to England 13/3.	—	Amaury, Lord of Cyprus.
1195	Richard recrowned.	Philip offers to make peace.	Greek attempt to regain Cyprus.
1196	Richard's war in France.	—	Latin Church instituted.
1197	Richard builds Chateau Gaillard.	War between France and England.	Amaury crowned king of Cyprus.
1198	—	Richard and Philip make peace.	Amaury marr. Isabella of Jerusalem, and becomes king of Jerusalem and Cyprus.
1199	Richard dies 6/4.	—	—

CYPRUS UNDER AN ENGLISH KING.

CHAPTER I.

THE Third Crusade had its origin in a variety of obscure political influences, far removed from the religious enthusiasm—or as some may be inclined to say—fanaticism, usually associated with such movements. At the same time it was ostensibly animated by religious zeal. In the twelfth century religion was to a great extent under the influence of political intrigues, and politics were intimately bound up with pious sentiment.

It was the most romantic episode of its kind in the course of mediæval history, reviving at the same time the religious ideals of the altruistic Godfrey and the fanatical Peter the Hermit of a century earlier.

The three great Crusades of the twelfth century were equidistant in date by a space of about fifty years. Each differed from the others: the first had been perhaps almost entirely religious enthusiasm; in the second the motives actuating Louis VII. and his remarkable wife the "Rose of Acquitaine," and the astute St. Bernard of Clairvaux had a great deal to do with the initiation of a French interest in the Levant which has endured from that day to this. In the third of these great movements a curious political *raison d'etre* evinces itself under the cloak of religion, which is not very easy to define.

The ostensible reason for the Crusade was the recovery of the Holy Land from the power of the Saracens : at the same time the statesmen of the great European powers were influenced by a curious policy which is referred to by the chroniclers, the policy that peace between the different nations, exhausted by the interminable warfare of the period, might most easily be secured by the absence of their respective feudal heads.[1]

In 1187, Pope Urban III. carrying on the traditional policy of his immediate predecessors in contest with the secular or temporal powers of Europe, was about to excommunicate the Emperor Frederick I. (Barbarossa) when suddenly the news of the capture of Jerusalem and the terrible disaster to the Christians at the battle of Tiberias in the month of September, arrived in Europe. The aged Pope is said to have been taken ill with grief at the receipt of this news: on October 17th he died. His successor, the short lived Gregory VIII., quickly abandoned the policy of excommunicating European sovereigns for an effort to unite them with himself against the common enemy already overwhelming the Holy Land, and the frontiers of European civilization on its eastern horizon.

A galley painted black, and with black sails denoting grief, sailed into the port of Marseilles early in the winter of 1187-88. On board was William, Archbishop of Tyre, the famous chronicler of the Crusades, bringing confirmation of the sad news. Archbishop William, on his arrival, lost no time in assisting Gregory VIII. in his efforts to initiate a Crusade which should unite all Europe in a campaign to rescue the Latin Kingdom of the Holy Land from the power of the infidels. His greatest gain was, perhaps, to secure the English King's son, Richard Cœur de Lion, then Count of Poitou, as his chief supporter.[2]

The Count of Poitou was almost the first to sign himself with the Cross, at the beginning of 1188, and his example was quickly followed by vast numbers of feudal seigneurs, and the commonalty all over Western Europe.

Immediately after the death of Henry II. in the following summer, and his own coronation as King of England (3rd September, 1189) King Richard set on foot the necessary preparations for a great military expedition, and the first levies of the Third Crusade were being raised throughout

[1] Vinsauf, II. 3.   [2] Ibid. II. 3.

AN ENGLISH KING. 3

the vast Anglo-Norman dominions which then extended from the half of Ireland, over the greater part of modern France, down to the frontier of Spain.[1]

Meanwhile the Emperor Frederick I. had started off on a crusade of his own, in spite of his 70 years of age. He had taken part in the Second Crusade of forty years before and although he was one of the last to sign himself with the Cross on this new quest, he was the first to appear in the field with an immense army of Germans which he had collected at Ratisbon. He took the way through Constantinople and Asia Minor, and after encountering endless difficulties due to the hostility of the Greeks, met with his death in endeavouring to ford the river Saleph (Selesius) in Cilicia. Without their emperor, the Germans dispersed, and few of them took part in the Crusade of 1191.[2]

The pact between the kings of England and France, by which they both agreed to be absent from their dominions at the same period, had been settled for a considerable time. Delay had occurred owing to Richard's succession to the English throne, and to the death of the Queen of France. But at last the English fleet of transports was despatched to Marseilles to await the arrival of the Crusading army marching overland.

In the beginning of the year 1190, the two kings met within the walls of the Abbey of Vezelay, that famous building which seems to have been regarded as the proper birthplace for several of the crusades, and whose embattled walls and gateways still survive as a *monument historique*. Here with customary pomp and magnificence they were received by the monks, each king with his immediate retainers being lodged in a separate part of the enormous Abbey without inconveniencing the regular monastic inhabitants. King Richard had arrived from Tours, in those days a city of the Anglo-Norman dominions, the French king Philip II., had journeyed from Paris, and the two allied monarchs, after a brief sojourn proceeded to Lyons where an encampment of some weeks had been arranged.

The great Benedictine Abbey of Vezelay had been the scene of strange events in the middle of the past century. There the " Rose of Acquitaine," the mother of Richard Cœur de Lion when Queen of France, had listened with her then husband, Louis VII. to the persuasive preaching

[1] Map in Bright's "Hist. of Eng."   [2] Gibbon, XI. 105.

of St. Bernard, on that eventful 31st of March, 1145. Then had followed the famous scene of enthusiasm, the shouting of the people demanding the "Cross" wherewith to mark

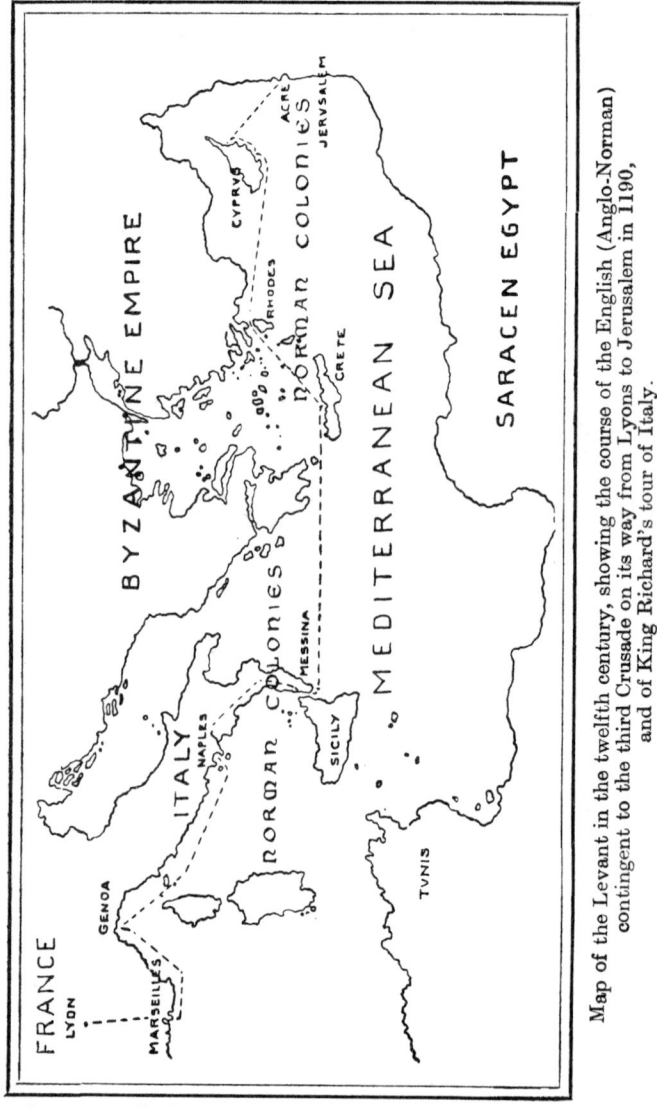

Map of the Levant in the twelfth century, showing the course of the English (Anglo-Norman) contingent to the third Crusade on its way from Lyons to Jerusalem in 1190, and of King Richard's tour of Italy.

themselves, and the tearing up of St. Bernard's cloak to make into the required badges.

AN ENGLISH KING. 5

And now in the footsteps of the "Rose of Acquitaine," the heroine of many a strange story during intervening years, stood her famous son, contemplating precisely the same expedition as that which had proved somewhat disastrous to his mother's reputation fifty years before : and with him was Louis VIIth's son by another wife. One might fancy them somewhat in the position of "brothers," although there was no blood relationship between them : and as the only kings of England and France who ever joined their forces in a military expedition as allies they were remarkable in the history of their respective countries.

In the early summer of 1190, A.D., the beautiful city of Lyons presented a gay scene to the eyes of its citizens, and to the numberless strangers thronging its picturesque old streets and quays on the banks of the Rhone. Fluttering pennons and swelling standards above innumerable tents marked the presence of a vast mediæval army camped in the green meadows around the city walls. Here the feudal lords of half Europe, each surrounded by his vassals and retainers, and marshalled with all the punctilious etiquette of the period, were met together to begin the great emprise of defending the Holy Kingdom of Jerusalem and the Sepulchre of Christ from the ever recurring usurpation by eastern infidels.

Military camps were common enough sights in the twelfth century, but this particular one had something unique about it. For obvious reasons there was a religious aspect and atmosphere, and an auxiliary army of priests and monks was partly occupying it. Vast numbers of pilgrims were taking advantage of the movement of a great army eastwards to gain certain facilities of transport, and more especially the protection afforded by numbers. The usual crowd of camp followers, always an important and unwelcome addition to a mediæval army was also present.

Although the two military Orders of monks formed a very large portion of the assembled army, the ecclesiastics were hardly distinguishable from their lay brethren, all were alike arrayed in the chain mail hauberks of the period, when prepared for battle ; at other times a leathern jerkin or linen surcoat usually covered a smaller mail shirt to protect the wearer from the assassin's knife. The life of the monk in camp was in conformity with the rules of his Order—or was supposed to be—but in the field his garb and duties were much the same as those of other soldiers.

In several places amongst the tent-groups temporary open-air altars with their appurtenances of crosses and lamps had been erected, and the occasional figure of a worshipper repeating his prayers with a chaplet of huge beads in his hands reminded the observer of the particular intention of this camp.

Trains of baggage waggons, loaded with provender, or with the heavier arms of warfare in use at this period, were arranged corral fashion in a way to divide the different sections, or " quarters " of the camp from each other, and thus assist in preventing the faction fights so apt to break out between the excitable and unruly elements of such a very mixed assemblage.

On two hillocks near the river, the royal standards of France and of Normandy floated from flagstaffs in the centres of four-wheeled waggons, at the sides of pavilions forming the respective headquarters of the King of France Philip II. (Augustus) and the Duke of Normandy and King of England Richard I. (Cœur de Lion).

Councils of war, the issuing of army regulations, the business of the commissariat, all the endless details of such a vast undertaking had more than filled the few weeks during which the camp had been stationed at Lyons, waste of time being caused by the intrigues of those seeking to occupy positions of a lucrative or important character. At last the arrival of the greater contingents, and the general conclusion of preparations imperatively demanded the break up of the camp and the marching of the army. At this juncture a slight difficulty arose : it had been stipulated by the two kings that neither should proceed without the other, but the difficulty of transporting so great an army was a serious impediment. It was therefore at length arranged that the King of France should be the first to leave Lyons by way of Genoa, where he had a contract for his transport by sea with the Superb Republic, the King of England proceeding by way of Marseilles. Both kings were to arrive in Messina about the month of September, 1190.

The King of France whose section of the great camp appears to have been on the eastern side of the Rhone,

AN ENGLISH KING. 7

proceeded on his way to pass the Alpes Maritimes in good order, but what might have been a serious mishap occurred when the larger section of the army, including the Anglo-Normans, began its march southwards. Desiring to cross over to the eastern side of the Rhone where the high road by way of Valence seems to have followed very much the line of the present railway to Marseilles, the troops with their baggage trains and heavy camp furniture had to pass by a wooden bridge. This bridge not destined for such a use suddenly gave way and precipitated about one hundred men into the river where it is of a rapid and violent course. But owing probably to the low water of summer in the river, all these men managed to get out save two who were drowned, " and " as the old chronicler says " experienced death of the body, though they live spiritually with Christ, in whose service they were." This mishap delayed the march for several days, but the King of England, if not the greatest general of his age, was remarkable for his genius in military engineering, immediately on hearing of the accident, collected together a number of boats, with which he made a floating bridge, over which the rest of the army was easily transported.[1]

The total numbers of the army which had made its rendezvous at Lyons in the spring and early summer of 1190 is supposed to have amounted to about 100,000 men.[2]

Our chief informant of all that took place in the adventurous journey of Richard Cœur de Lion on his famous crusade, is a man who was the eyewitness of the events he describes. A member of a religious Order—probably Benedictine—he appears to have been young and active, and to have appreciated the splendours of the mediæval panoply of war, to have observed with care the circumstances of the countries through which the way led, to have been filled with admiration for the hero of the expedition. This learned monk refrains from much criticism of the political life of his day, he found like most of his contemporaries, or for that matter like most people born into a settled state of society such as that of feudalism with its daily obligations and somewhat mechanical occupations, that a spirit of contentment still lingered over the European world. The great upheaval of the thirteenth and fourteenth centuries was yet to come. A Francis and Dominic had not appeared with their revolutionary ideals and Christian

([1]) Vinsauf. II. 10.   ([2]) Ibid. II. 9.

philanthropy to disturb the natural current of human life. The frightful increase of population had not yet begun to cause the poverty of overcrowded cities, the miseries of the overburdened country-side belong to a later age. Following as a pilgrim, with the permission of his monastic superior, in the great army of fanatics and adventurers, our author was to have a pleasant and interesting experience: he was to witness events of real romance and of far reaching importance, events which to us moderns seem almost incredible, and which are yet clearly enough historical although centering for the most part in the personality of an individual. He was a Norman, a member of that virile race whose name is associated with that sentiment of superiority, that directness of purpose which is generally so successful in the conduct of all affairs. Fair and fresh of appearance, with the aquiline features and blue eyes of the North, he presented much that was in contrast with dark complexioned Provençal or Gascon brethren of his Order with whom chance threw him in the course of his travels. A slight difference in the cut of his monastic garb from that more usual in the southern countries emphasized his foreign origin.

Master Geoffrey the Cellararius—such was his title as dimly recorded in those traces of him which have descended to us through seven centuries—occupied a position of eminence in his Order. The Cellararius or Cellarer was the highest dignitary of a Benedictine Abbey, next the Abbot. He was the steward of its temporalities, and controlled all that appertained to the well-being of a monastery outside the spiritual or more strictly religious character which came under the particular care of the Abbot. The Cellarer was usually a man of education and business habits, on whom devolved the whole care of the community, and in the present case he was also a man of literary tastes, and at least ten of his books on different subjects are known to survive in a manuscript form.[1] His account of the adventures of Richard Cœur de Lion is full of interesting details, more especially in that portion which deals with the passage of the crusaders through the Greek region of the Levant beginning at the Straits of Messina.

[1] Geoffrey de Vinsauf's numerous writings include : The Itinerary of Richard I. An appeal to the Emperor Henry VI., for liberating King Richard. A Monody on Richard's death. Works on Rhetoric, Ethics and Poetry, and a book which may perhaps have given him his name of Vinsauf, entitled " Management of vineyards, fruit treees, grafting, etc."

AN ENGLISH KING. 9

The journey from Lyons to Marseilles of the Anglo-Norman contingent occupied some days, and was diversified by a sight of objects of an extraordinary interest. The remains of ancient Rome scattered along the route, which carried them through the loveliest scenery of southern France, would perhaps attract but little attention, but the old castle of Rochemaure, probably in existence at that time, with its bridges spanning the surrounding abysses, would appeal to the military taste of the period. Then as the army approached Orange it must have marched beneath the Roman triumphal arch spanning the road, in strange historical contrast with the Latin soldiery for whose glorification the monument had been erected more than a millenium before. Avignon, in another century to become famous as the city of the Popes, was still a small old Roman town of comparatively little importance, basking in the summer sunshine amongst its vine-clad hills and olive groves.

And all along the way the camp life of a great mediæval army had to be maintained. The long day's dusty march ending in a settlement for the night in such places as were considered most convenient, with the grandly picturesque scenery of the Rhone valley lighted up with scores of camp fires and flaring torches forming the background to a sufficiently wild and impressive scene. The beautiful characteristics of French river-side scenery, its seigneural residences and busy cleanly towns upon the water side, afforded infinite pleasure to the Norman monk whose life had hitherto been spent in that comparatively sullen land of the north, that land of misty skies where the sun seemed to travel in half-hearted fashion along the horizon, instead of rising triumphantly into the heavens overhead. To him the vine-clad hills, the clear atmosphere, the brilliant sun, formed a revelation of the beauty of the world which had been difficult to realize within the austere precincts of his northern monastery.

The incidents of the march down the side of the great river were attractive to a speculative mind. The contrast between the high strung principles and the inadequate practice of such a marvellous creation as the feudal law, was exemplified in a thousand ways : the mutual dependence of lord upon vassal, of inferior upon superior, was clearly enough maintained, but at the same time many of those unfortunate qualities in our human nature which like ill weeds are for ever springing up, were equally evident. Then the maintaining a sufficient control over many of the wilder spirits in such a vast assemblage of armed men seemed beyond all human organization. The region through which they passed had not received such a visitation for fifty years, and the poor country people for miles around the route fled, if they were wise, carrying away or concealing their stores of wheat and wine, abandoning their cottages to a deplorable fate.

CHAPTER II.

The outward pomp and ceremony of feudalism was singularly emphasized in all appertaining to the person of the sovereign prince : ritual ceremonial in modern days is associated more especially with a religious sentiment and display—in the middle ages it was equally shown in the smallest details connected with the daily life of kings, and even the frank and bluff manners with which Richard Plantagenet is credited were probably but occasional lapses from the decorum and burdensome court etiquette with which his existence was saddled. All records that we have surviving of Cœur de Lion seem to suggest that his inner nature would very naturally rebel against the shackles of a most conventional formalism—such a formalism as would in some degree represent the treatment of an Egyptian Pharoah or a Chinese Emperor within their palace-temples. From such a course of life it must have been a marvellous pleasure to the great king when he escaped into the open country under an excuse of warfare, and still more when that escape seemed likely to extend over the long period of a crusade. But even under such circumstances the iron-bound regulations of the feudal state must follow the feudal lord on his journey. As an instance amongst others of the wearisome ceremonial attending the movements of the king, which attracted Master Geoffrey's attention like everything else about a court with which he had made his first acquaintance at Lyons, was the manner in which the royal meals were served. It must be remembered that even so late as the nineteenth century the dinner in public of a prince survived as a custom and was even restored by Louis XVIII. and Charles X. Richard Plantagenet was compelled by the same custom to dine in public, and being a bachelor to take his meal entirely alone.

As Master Geoffrey stood on the turf of the open space surrounding the royal tents, attracted by the sight of a crowd of spectators awaiting, about midday, the spectacle of the royal repast, he presently saw a small body of men-at-arms, their helmets and coats of mail glittering in the sun, approach the entrance of the king's pavilion. A space was then formed to keep the spectators at a distance by guards stationed around under the instructions of a quartermaster. In due course appeared varlets carrying a table on iron legs, covered with a cloth—a species of tray with sides, resembling the modern "dumbwaiter," on which beneath the cloth were the bread and meat and a small knife. The quartermaster then cried in a sonorous voice "Messieurs ! la viande du roi !" at which all the assemblage of spectators uncovered their heads. Richard then appeared on the scene, issuing from his tent door, and took his seat on a kind of folding chair of elaborate wrought metalwork, whilst the *somellier* or butler and various squires took up their appointed places. The squire-carver now made his appearance, he washed his hands in a bowl held by one of the assistants, and dried them on a towel provided by another.

In the hands of one of the attendant varlets was a small chalice, within which lay the horn of a rhinoceros, supposed to be a sovereign charm against poison : this played an important part in the mediæval table service under the name "licorne."[1]

The squire-carver having approached the royal table immediately the prince had seated himself, proceeded to turn down the cloth covering it. He then took up the napkin lying with the bread, and having kissed it ceremoniously, presented it to the prince. He then removed the napkin in which the bread was wrapped, and having shaken it, placed it around his own neck so that the two ends hung down in front. Then he took the bread in his left hand—his hand being covered with the napkin which was about his neck—and with a large knife cut the loaf in two pieces, one of which he caused a varlet to hold whilst he applied the horn of the rhinoceros to all its parts "pour faire l'essai." The bread was then cut into slices, and placed before the king together with the small knife, which it was also necessary that the squire-carver should kiss ceremoniously on the handle before placing in the king's hands.

It was the duty of the squire-carver carefully to examine and test all the utensils, such as plates or knives, to touch them with his lips, and to taste all the dishes provided

(1) Viollet le Duc.

AN ENGLISH KING. 13

for the royal table. The idea of poison was an all-pervading terror in the mediæval world, and such an idea was justified by the frequency with which the crimes of the poisoner were perpetrated in private or political life. Even the knife handles and napkins used at table were suspected of being channels for the purpose.

The succession of dishes at a royal table was very much in the order usually followed at the present day. Potage or soup was the opening course, then came the omelette or fish as the second dish, and the chief *plat* of the roasted or fried meat was followed by pastry, sweetmeats, and fruit. Each of the courses was presented on the table covered with a napkin which was removed with the same ceremonial of examination, kissing, tasting, etc., and with the application of the licorne or other potent charm against poison approved of by popular opinion. Forks being as yet but rarely used in the service of the table, both the squire-carver and the prince he served, made use of their fingers for the purpose, and as a rule the morsels or slices cut off a joint were placed upon slabs of bread as a substitute for plates. We seem to see a similar primitive mode surviving amongst rustics of comparatively modern days when eating their midday meal of bread and bacon in the fields. In dealing with a joint of meat or a bird the squire-carver would cut it up into portions on a silver platter reserving what was not eaten by the seigneur either for himself, or for distribution amongst the poor. Such was the laborious and tedious feeding of a sovereign prince in the twelfth century, a public spectacle upon which Master Geoffrey the monk turned his inquisitive gaze amongst many other curious features in the life of the period.[1]

At Marseilles, Master Geoffrey found but little to attract his notice, his attention was fully occupied with the troubles and anxieties of getting a place on board one of the larger transports intended to convey the troops and all the impedimenta of an army to the Straits of Messina. It was the middle of August and the heat was great, the mosquitoes troublesome, and the sooner the fleet began to move southwards the better. But notwithstanding these inducements to a speedy departure he was detained at this port for three weeks. Here within the famous harbour which has

[1] Viollet le Duc.

in all ages conferred so much importance on the greatest mediæval and modern commercial city of the Mediterranean were the ships destined to convey the English crusaders. From the margin of the harbour, lined with quays, the ground was thickly covered with squalid houses, warehouses, and the residences of the richer merchants, crowded together amongst narrow lanes, as if for mutual protection, the whole forming an amphitheatre terminating in the encircling chain of hills crowned by battlemented walls and towers. At that time the port was offensive from the filth draining into it on account of the conformation of the ground, and the stagnation of the tideless sea water. A visitor was lucky if he escaped the consequences of such unhealthy conditions, which to a resident seemed curiously a matter of indifference.

During his enforced stay in Marseilles, Master Geoffrey made one or two excursions outside the city walls, but the open country in the height of summer was sufficiently uninviting: a sky of copper, an atmosphere loaded with dust, the scorching sun with its lurid glare parching the arid earth—was hardly attractive. Like the dry bones of some wasted corpse, the bare rocky hills rise above the surface with a sombre melancholy sternness, their barren summits of grey stone causing the eyes to ache or to seek in vain for some patch of green. Provence, the land of poetry and romance possesses a landscape which seems singularly inappropriate to such ideas: the troubadours and minstrels seem to have flourished in their favourite haunt in spite of very adverse surroundings. The people of the city and its district were also unpleasing to the more refined and educated northerner, their fervid temperament partaking of the fiery atmosphere and the heated soil of a southern clime was unsympathetic to his colder nature. Rude in manner, of an aspect which is often forbidding and sinister, and speaking a harsh patois unintelligible both to French and Normans, but resembling a bastard Italian or Catalan dialect, he could have but little communication with them beyond the limited chaffering of the market necessary for daily necessities. As a member of the Benedictine Order, Master Geoffrey had been received as a very welcome guest in the great Abbey of St. Victor, one of the most celebrated houses of his rule, which at the time of his visit was being rebuilt

AN ENGLISH KING.

in the new style of art with its pointed arches, and soaring vaults—seeming to mark the beginning of those changes coming over the world, those elements of discontent with the older order which stamp the thirteenth century with its particular character. Yet whilst noting the presence of new art-fashions in the general design of the great church, Master Geoffrey was interested to observe that some features of an older type seemed to survive like older growth of wild flowers surviving amongst newly turned furrows. The chevron and the dogtooth ornaments still maintained their places amongst the delicately studied play of light and shadow on the mouldings of the developing Gothic style. A Norman eye was of necessity keenly critical in all new architectural developments, for had not the Norman monks of England been the greatest architects in the world for more than a hundred years.

The English ships which had taken months to make the passage round to Marseilles by way of the Pillars of Hercules, were at length arrived in readiness to transport the Anglo-Norman contingent on its voyage to Acre. This fleet consisted of fourteen great " dromons " or ships of the largest size then known, approximating to the form and dimensions of a modern frigate, and of about one hundred smaller craft, galleys, tartanas or feluccas. The larger vessels carried the horses of value, trained to warfare, with all their grooms and attendant varlets, besides a considerable supply of food for men and animals, their arms and accoutrements. The king's treasure which was considerable and which had been extorted in many dubious ways all over his dominions, had to be disposed of amongst the various ships of the fleet, so that should disaster befall, the whole of it would not be sacrificed in any particular vessel.

The knights and seigneurs of the expedition followed the example of the King of England in securing galleys for their transport instead of the slow sailing larger ships. In this way they were able to proceed in a more independent manner, and stay at seaside towns along the route, where they were sure of an agreeable entertainment and a hearty welcome. These galleys were propelled both by oars and sails, whilst the noble passengers occupied the quarter-deck with its cabin and awnings; on the great lateen sails were painted the armorials of the seigneur, or the figure of some patron saint ; in the forecastle stood the men-at-arms and the musicians, whilst gay pennons and banners fluttered from every mast and spar. Each galley presented a spectacle more suggestive of a festal progress than would be possible to associate with our modern ideas of warfare, and as their approach was heralded by the sound of drums and trumpets they produced a sensation in every port on the coasts of Corsica and Sardinia past which their course was set.

The final arrangements for departure being completed, and the horses—a most important feature in the equipage—having been duly introduced into the ships' holds through a door, or great porthole in their sides, which had afterwards to be carefully closed and caulked to keep it watertight, an order for embarkation was issued by King Richard.

On many of the ships were numbers of priests and monks, some of whom were going on pilgrimage, others as fighting men, for in those days there were no religious disabilities or prejudices on the part of the clergy against bloodshed in the cause of the Holy Land. When the priests and clerks had embarked, the captains of the ships insisted upon their holding a religious service on the quarter-decks, and chanting appropriate psalms and antiphons with a view to obtain a prosperous voyage. The beautiful hymn of " Veni Creator " with its solemn Gregorian tone, resounded through the fleet whilst the mariners hauled in the anchors, and spread their canvas to the favouring breeze. As the sails of the square rigged larger ships, and the long lateens of the galleys began to fill, and the whole fleet, headed by the royal galleys, was leaving the harbour on its seaward course of many adventures, on that August day of more than seven hundred years ago, the sight was singularly impressive, it was also singularly romantic. The object in view for most of the participators in the Third Crusade was to realize a strange religious ideal, others may have been animated by ambition, or the love of adventure, or even by mere sordid aims, but in any case the result of all this display of many sided human endeavour could not but furnish material for a series of the greatest episodes of mediæval history.

Crowds of spectators naturally lined the heights surrounding the mouth of the famous harbour of Marseilles, where in modern days the cathedral has been built, and on the opposite side which then was occupied by the fortress of St. Nicholas, or the " Rock " as it was called, and mingled their shouts and cries of adieu with the sounds of sacred and secular music proceeding from the departing ships. Amongst these spectators not a few women participated in the ceremony of farewell : some attracted by the presence on board the fleet of members of their own sex who were accompanying husbands or lovers on this great adventure, others were there to wave their goodbyes to the northern acquaintances of a few past weeks, the handsome youthful seigneurs and squires who were departing in all the pride of life, clad in the panoply of splendid mediæval warfare, and doomed for the most part never to return.

As the summer evening began to close over the beautiful Gulf of Lyons and its group of islands through which the last ships of the departing fleet—the laggard slow sailing transports—were disappearing on their way south, the strains of music, the lessening long drawn notes of clarion and trumpet were borne upon the breeze like the echo of a forlorn hope. Once more after fifty years had Marseilles witnessed the passing through her port of the chivalry of Western Europe bent upon another struggle with that mighty and invincible power in the Near East which represented the impenetrable and unknown potentialities of the vast Moslem world. Once more were the fields of Palestine to be the arena dyed with blood, for the display of prowess by western heroes, and the capricious magnanimity of eastern despots. The sacrifice of countless lives on either side of the great struggle over a mere religious sentiment, which to our modern minds would be almost unintelligible, has sanctified such a page of history and its complex motives and aims seem almost beyond our cynical criticism. With the disappearance of the last of the English ships the pageant of a great Crusade such as the world will never see again, had passed into the gathering shadows of the night—into the mere records of the past, and into an oblivion which is somewhat difficult to penetrate in these modern days.[1]

[1] Our learned Benedictine, Geoffrey the Cellarer, having obtained a passage for himself, and his servant-brother on board one of the transports which was sailing direct to Messina by way of the Straits of Bonifazio, could but have given a hearsay account of King Richard's adventures amongst the Normans of Calabria—this is supplemented by the Chronicle of Roger de Howden (or Hoveden).

Warship of the twelfth century.

CHAPTER III.

The royal galley of King Richard, accompanied by two others as an escort had been the first to leave the port of Marseilles but instead of following the course of the main fleet and the transports, through the Straits of Bonifazio between Corsica and Sardinia, it had been steered along the Riviera coast in a straight line for the great port of Genoa.

Urged by the oars of a chosen band of rowers the royal galley with its heraldic blazonings on sails and hull of the two lions of Normandy : its canvas full bellied with the western breeze, made excellent progress, and at dawn of the third day following the departure from Marseilles, the beautiful mountain range of the Italian Riviera was rapidly becoming more distinct. Soon the lighthouse flare of the famous pharos of Genoa could be seen across the yellow waves and the dark purple shadows of daybreak, and within a few hours the English ships were entering the famous port, with all their banners and ensigns displayed.

Due notification was made to the civil and ecclesiastical authorities on shore of the arrival of the royal galleys with the king on board, and forthwith a fitting welcome was

AN ENGLISH KING. 19

immediately ordered to be prepared. Bells clanged overhead, carpets and hangings were displayed from every window in the excessively tall houses which make the narrow lanes of the city so cool and twilit even at noon on the hottest day. Clarions, trumpets and drums resounded on every side whilst processions of clergy from the different " collegiate " carrying their reliquaries on their shoulders and swinging censers were preparing to move down to the landing place.

At the base of the great lighthouse stood the officials of the Republic, the senators in their purple robes, the prelates of high rank and the canons of the cathedral ready to conduct the king into the presence of the " consul " or supreme chief of the State, and the archbishop in their respective palaces.

A processional escort having been formed on the quay, the King of England was first led to the cathedral, which at that time was being rebuilt with the curious horizontal stripes of black and white marble as we see in its older portions at the present day ; a style of architecture only permitted in public edifices of the commune or of the four great families, Doria, Grimaldi, Spinola, and Fieschi. At its west door was stationed the archbishop in his cope and mitre, who conducting Cœur de Lion to a faldstool in front of the great rood-screen, proceeded to celebrate pontifical mass. At the conclusion of the liturgy the ceremony of exposing the great relics of the church for adoration took place. The famous " Catino " or glass bowl, supposed at one time to be cut out of an enormous emerald, and regarded as having been used at the " Last Supper " was brought in its reliquary from the treasury, and the king was permitted to touch it with his lips whilst the " clavigeri " or hereditary guardians of the much revered relic stood around.[1]

Then rising from his knees after the adoration of the sacred relics, the king was conducted by the senators, accompanied by crowds of citizens, to the Palazzo Pubblico, where the consul awaited his coming, clad in his robes of State and with a cap of maintenance on his head.

The lord of the Genoese Republic surrounded by the princely senators stood at the foot of the grand staircase

[1] The " Sacro Catino " is fully described by Sir Martin Conway : " Antiquaries Journal " IV., ii.

within the court of the Palazzo Pubblico, and Cœur de Lion, clad in his royal robes with the fleur de lisé crown on his head, was thence led into the great council chamber on the upper floor or *piano nobile*. Seated on two raised seats, whilst the senators sat on benches against the walls, the consul and the king carried on a lengthy debate on certain political questions which evidently arose from the recent passage of the French king and his forces through Genoa. The proceedings were however brought to a close in the most friendly manner and the king having promised to favour the claims of the Genoese Republic in preference to those of Venice, Pisa, or Amalfi, valuable financial assistance was promised in return.

Grimaldo Grimaldi, Prince of Monaco, Marquis and Count, and High Admiral of the Holy Roman Empire was consul or supreme lord of the Republic of Genoa in 1162, 1170, and 1184. His son Obert Grimaldi succeeded him as consul and admiral in 1197, but it is not quite certain which occupied the position in 1190 at the time of Cœur de Lion's visit. In either case the Grimaldi would receive him with warmest welcome, and do all that was possible towards the furtherance of the Crusade, for Obert Grimaldi had been a main agent in its inception and encouragement. He had attended the coronation ceremony of Richard in September, 1189, on behalf of both the Emperor and of the King of France to urge the claims and advantages of the proposed Crusade. This occasioned the holding of the first Parliament at Westminster of barons, earls, and bishops, that had been held in England since the Norman Conquest, and at this meeting the Crusade was definitely agreed upon.

Frederick, the younger brother of Obert Grimaldi, was grand master of the cross-bowmen of the King of England, in which office he appears to have joined the Crusade.

Here it must be noted that the Genoese were particularly famed in the middle ages for proficiency in the use of the crossbow. One hundred and fifty years after the time of the Third Crusade, the Genoese cross-bowmen were employed as mercenaries against the English at Crécy and Poitiers under another Grimaldi, Prince of Monaco.

A magnificent palace—one of the many which then decorated the city—was prepared for the king's lodging.

Here during his stay the usual banquets and entertainments to which all the nobles and great merchant princes found their way were given in the king's honour. To be the guest of an Italian Republic in the middle ages was always a memorable experience—to be the guest of the Superb Republic had no parallel in such entertainment.

"Genova la Superba," the capital city of the Ligurian Republic was the most powerful of all commercial communities of that period. Its only rivals were Venice on the one hand, and Marseilles on the other.

The Genoese Republic had found the crusades of the past hundred years particularly profitable, ever since it had been acting as the first of "army contractors" in the port of St. Simeon, during the first siege of Antioch (1099) supplying food and wine from Cyprus and other parts of the Byzantine Empire, and keeping up communications with Europe. Then had been obtained the treaties and capitulations by which the Republic had quarters assigned to its merchants, with all manner of privileges, in all the Levantine towns. The capture of the small but important town and port of Djebail or Giblet near Tripoli by the Genoese Hugh de Lembriac in 1108, laid the foundation for further enterprise of the same kind in Syria and Palestine. The agents or bailiffs of the Republic became in a few more years the most important of the many functionaries and official representatives of European wealth and commerce who crowded the market places and ports of the Levant, and their privileged courts of justice and their viscounts were recognised even in the interior of Armenia.

At the period of Cœur de Lion's visit the vast organization called the Bank of St. George was in its infancy, but the King of England was doubtless glad to take advantage of such a valuable support to his credit as a banking account with the wealthiest government of his period naturally afforded.

Even in those days the great families of the Grimaldi, Doria, Spinola, Fieschi, and a hundred other famous names, were living in their huge palaces amongst the narrow crowded lanes, with all the pomp and state of a wealthy oligarchy controlling vast commercial interests. The huge "fondacci" of the middle ages had probably already come into existence with their curious corporations of the privileged "Facchini di Confidenza" and their laws prohibiting an entrance into the great warehouses of any soldier, priest, or woman—the three classes of the community which seemed equally liable to suspicion.

Beneath the tall archway of the Porta Vacca (Cowgate) near the "fondacci," which had been built in 1150, and which still survives as a wonderful landmark of those ancient times, the King of England must have passed on his arrival and departure. Over this gateway appeared the red cross badge of the Republic, and the statue of its patron saint George. The similarity with the red crosses with which King Richard had marked himself and his men suggested the adoption by the Anglo-Normans of the same soldier saint as their national patron, and from henceforth the red cross badge and the war-cry "Saint George Aie" became the distinctions alike of English and Genoese on the field of battle ; or the flag of a merchant ship or galley.

The departure of the King of England from Genoa was again the occasion of due ceremonial and appropriate observances by the officials of the "Superb Republic." Once more the senators in their purple robes, the ecclesiastical dignitaries with their sacred emblems and reliquaries assembled at the royal lodging and conducted Richard and his suite to the place of embarkation near the "fondacci," whilst the ringing of bells, and the drums and trumpets of the civic guards proclaimed the importance of the event. After the usual benedictions by the clergy and the distribution of largesse by the royal treasurer, the king stepped on board his galley .amidst the shouts of an enthusiastic multitude on the shore of the port, and in a short time was out at sea on a course due south, skirting the lovely scenery of the Italian Riviera.

Soon the entrancing view of the Gulf of Luna (now known as Spezia) came on the port side of the galley ; here the bold headland crowned by the temple of Venus which had recently been converted into a church, and surrounded by walls and towers, constituting the frontier fortress of Porto Venere, formed the last landmark of the Superb Republic.

On the day following the king's departure from Genoa, the islands of the Tuscan archipelago began to show upon the southern horizon. Capraja, Elba, Monte Christo, and

AN ENGLISH KING. 23

Gorgona were passed in succession towards eventide, but at that period these islands were scarcely inhabited, except by a few pirates and fishermen whose occupancy would be occasionally disturbed by battles between Genoese and Pisan fleets or the presence of Saracen rovers on the lookout for slaves.

The royal galleys continued their southerly course, steering away from the land in order to avoid any encounter with Pisan or Gaetan corsairs, who might possibly venture to attack any ships which appeared to be detached from the company of the main crusading fleet. Far away on the port bow lay the islands of Ponza, and Palmarola, behind which rose the imposing Monte Circello, famous as the mythical island of Circe, and the grand headland crowned with the ancient city of Gaeta, now in its last years of existence as a Republic. On the extreme horizon lay the majestic mountains of the southern Abruzzi serving as a background covered with the misty lights and shadows of early autumn.

Richard viewed the beautiful scene with far-reaching thoughts: charmed with the distant prospect of blue mountains, the brilliance of the Tyrhennian Sea, covered with its sparkling wavelets, he seemed to be passing through a natural paradise, but at the same time he knew it to be a region where Greek and Saracen, Frank and Latin, were wrestling in a death struggle for exclusive possession, and where his own Norman cousins were now assuming a supremacy which would tax all their energies to maintain. He doubtless realised the immense problem which was presented by this concourse of different races, the possibility of their fusion, or on the other hand the probability of that survival of the fittest which would most naturally occur to the energetic Norman of the twelfth century. He realised moreover that the relatively small numbers of Normans overlording the ever desirable Mediterranean shores would only be able to maintain their position so long as they retained the character of foreign conquerors, and the manners and customs of their northern forefathers— any fusion of themselves with natives meant their own extinction.

Soon after sunrise on the next day the royal galleys were rounding the beautiful island of Ischia on the port bow, whilst on the starboard side was Capri, lying like some huge opal on a sea of purple illumined by the clear morning light. The ever famous Bay of Naples stretched out in front, with the great volcano forming the centre of the scene : the strangest of natural phenomena to northern eyes. The galleys which during the night had been sailing on a gentle breeze, were once more trimmed for rowing ; the sweeps were got out and slipped into the rowlocks, and the ships made ready for entering port with their armories and banners displayed. The course being set due east they began to make way, heading for the land, and in a few hours were entering the port of Naples.

As the ships approached the city, the results of its comparatively recent conquest by the Norman princes of Apulia were very noticeable in the new buildings, and more especially in the frowning fortresses of the Castel Caprano and the Castel dell'Ovo, which were then in course of construction under the auspices of the Venetian Maestro Buono, the builder of the Campanile of St. Mark. The mighty round towers of the Norman " bastille " which seemed to embody the sentiment of a conquering and invincible race dominating the thickly populated city, were particularly impressive, and at the same time attracted the attention of King Richard because of his well known enthusiasm for military architecture. A certain resemblance between the Castel Caprano and the famous Chateau Gaillard may not improbably be due to this visit to Naples.

The King of England was received with all due honour by his Norman cousins of Apulia, Calabria and Sicily, then constituting the newly founded Kingdom of Naples and Sicily. The customary etiquette was observed with all its burdensome ceremonial and its long drawn-out compliments. The grand officials of the Neapolitan Kingdom escorted the English monarch to a specially prepared palace and the inevitable banquet took place that same day. Then as King Tancred was at the time residing at Palermo, King Richard shortly removed to Salerno, the seat of the great Norman university and school of medicine, where he stayed for some little time before making a tour of the Norman dominions of southern Italy by way of Melfi and Potenza to Scalea.

At Salerno King Richard found a more distinctly Norman population and surroundings, it was a place which

had been for long the main landing place in Italy of Norman
adventurers and colonists and the pilgrims for Palestine,
all of whom sought to avoid the uncongenial and often
hostile communities of " Griffons " as the inhabitants
of the decaying Byzantine Republics of Amalfi, Naples,
and Gaeta were called. It had also been for more than
a hundred years the chief port of the Normán Duchy of
Apulia and Calabria before the creation of the Neapolitan
Kingdom by King Roger and the barons within its walls
in 1130.

Whilst staying in Salerno King Richard visited the
monastery of Cava which had just been inaugurated.
In the entrance of the church stood the magnificent sarcophagus of Sibylla, wife of the great Roger; in its beautiful
cloister which still survives as Richard saw it was the tomb
of at least one pope. Within the neighbouring church
of Pietra Santa he would be shown the curious rock pro-
jecting through the floor before the altar where the First
Crusade was preached.

On the 13th of September King Richard departed from
Salerno on his tour of Calabria and Apulia.

Following the high road—it was of course a mere
beaten track worn into deep ruts by the hoofs of animals
and the feet of men in the course of endless ages and had
no resemblance to a modern high road—which from the
Paestum marshes leads up into the foothills of the southern
Apennines, the royal cavalcade pursued its way through
a rich country diversified by forest land and vineyards.
Farther on, although patches of forest filled the ravines,
the aspect of the mountains became bare and stony. The
castle of Muro stood above a ravine of the most wild and
dreary scenery. Then came a region where the miserable
villages betrayed the signs of the perpetually recurring
earthquake, and so on to the slopes of Monte Vultura with
its beds of lava and its forests. At Muro the royal party
was accommodated within the castle for the night.

After a long day's journey the city of Melfi was reached,
and as the sun was setting its last rays illumined the
picturesque buildings and spires, the crowded houses and
converts perched on the rock ridge with the towers of a
massive castle at its end. In the midst rose the fine

Norman cathedral the building of King William the Bad. Shady forests of chestnuts embowered the city rising into the thick woods which crown the neighbouring Monte Vultura.

The King of England with his escort of knights and servants rode with the clatter of horses and arms and the notes of a trumpet into the open space in front of the castle barbican. In a few minutes the bridge closing the door of the castle slowly descended across the rock-hewn moat, and rested on the stone curb on the opposite side, as the great counterpoise beams and chains which supported it were lowered, and the gate of the barbican was at the same time thrown open. The main gate in the castle wall which was disclosed to view by the fall of the drawbridge had been drawn back, and within its archway stood the seneschal of the fortress and his subordinate officers in readiness to welcome the king. At the same time the battlemented and machicolated walls on the entrance front of the castle were manned by the warders and sentinels.

The king and his horsemen then rode across the echoing wooden bridge, and the gothic archway in the castle wall seemed to devour them like some monstrous mouth, whilst the sinister looking arrowslits in the surrounding towers might be fancifully compared to reptile eyes on the watch.

Melfi was at this period one of the principal capitals of the Norman kingdom of Naples. It was here that in 1043, the Norman chiefs under William Bras de Fer, whom they had chosen as their head with the title of Count of Apulia, had convened a great council to determine the method of their new government in the chaos ruin of Byzantine and Lombard institutions following the Norman invasions. In the neighbouring town of Venosa was the Abbey of the Holy Trinity, wherein, as in a royal mausoleum the illustrious Norman brothers of the Hauteville family : William Bras de Fer, Drogo, Humphrey and Robert Guiscard, had been interred during the eleventh century—the last named whose body had been brought " non absque labor " from the island of Cephalonia, after the ship which bore it had been wrecked on the coast of Apulia.

AN ENGLISH KING. 27

More than one hundred and fifty years had passed away since the days when the sons of Tancred de Hauteville had aspired to change their condition as country squires of Normandy into being the kings of the richest countries of the southern sea. When Richard Cœur de Lion visited Naples and Melfi, the wonderful sea robbers and brigands who had pillaged stables and farmyards to supply their needs at their first appearance in Italy, and had lived to mate with princes and sway the politics of Europe with their swords, had been dead and buried for more than a century, but their descendants ruled the country still with a firm and vigorous hand.[1]

As the autumn night closed in on the Apennines and their scenery disappeared in the darkness, the small windows and arrowslits of the castle shone out with a curious effect of sparkling lights like great glow-worms in the distance. Within the castle a busy scene presented itself : in all its numerous chambers lamps and candles had been lighted and a suitable feast was being prepared for the illustrious strangers, with all that ambition for display which was so characteristic of mediæval life. The great vaulted hall in the centre of the fortress was illumined by coronas of metal supporting long candles arranged in a circular manner, and suspended from the rings in the vaulting bosses, whilst against the walls were fastened embroidered hangings below the wall passage which in a castle hall passed round at the level of the small windows beneath the vaulting. Against the sides of the hall were the long benches and narrow board tables as usual, whilst at the raised end under a canopy was the seat of the seigneurs, now to be occupied by the king.

Life in a mediæval castle was singularly like that of a community regulated by laws of etiquette and precedence. It resembled much more what we associate with the usages of a convent than anything we know of in ancient or classic times, or the domestic household of our Elizabethan

[1] A great Norman kingdom in the British Islands, Norman principalities in Italy, Sicily, Greece, and above all a Norman kingdom of Jerusalem and the nearer East proved the extraordinary force and virility of the famous race during the eleventh and twelfth centuries. Few of the other races of mankind have perhaps enjoyed the privilege or the opportunity of so rapid a development into so dominant a position as that of the earlier Normans, and certainly none ever availed themselves of such a development within so short a period.

forefathers in a later age. There may have been a certain
domesticity in the lives of castellans and chatelaines, but
the precincts of a feudal castle seem hardly to have been
the fitting milieu wherein to rear a large family. The
lord and his lady might live in their castle surrounded
by retainers and officials, but their children had often to
be relegated to the care of trusted feudatories in the form
of farmers or peasants in the neighbourhood.[1]

Richard spent but a day or two at Melfi, but he did
not omit to visit the exquisite scenery of the extinct
volcano of Monte Vultura. Amongst the tall trees surrounding the sparkling lake of Monticchio, on whose grassy
banks Horace had played when a child, he partook of an
al fresco meal. Here amid sylvan scenes which afforded
a pleasing change from the tedious ceremonial and etiquette
of a feudal castle and its gloomy enclosures, the king was
able to enjoy his ease amongst a few chosen retainers,

[1] From the remains which survive of the castles and habitations of our forefathers of the tenth and eleventh centuries (now, alas ! very rare fragments) one must suppose that they consisted of little more than fortified camps, with a substantial donjon in the midst ; the rest of the buildings being mere hamlet or village houses, where the members of the community lodged as well as they could amongst stables, kitchens, and storehouses, and trusted to a high wall of enclosure with a few towers for their security. But with the twelfth century and the crusades, a marked change comes over the appearance of the great feudal castles. The size of the donjon is much increased, and the subordinate buildings assume a greater importance ; less of a mere refuge in war time it becomes more of an ingeniously planned and permanent habitation for the feudal lord and his retainers.

Feminine emancipation and independence from a mere servile domesticity which had formerly constituted the existence of all women, was another very remarkable feature of Norman as distinguished from pre-Norman conditions of society. The presence of princesses and ladies of all degrees in the military camps of the Crusaders—although not without precedent in an earlier age—seemed to presage that general equalization in the status of the sexes which is often supposed to be peculiarly modern. In the fifteenth century the feminine element or influence in political and social life of what is called the " Age of Romance " culminated in such a heroine as Joan of Arc.

The finest and most remarkable example of the completed type of feudal chateau ever built is the famous one of Coucy in north-east France, the principal features of which were destroyed by the ruthless Germans in 1917. This marvellous building, which we know so much about from its preservation in the pages of Viollet le Duc, displays all the curious ingenuity of plan, together with economy of construction which came into existence in feudal times. Methods of defence, ways of escape, ingenuity in sanitation, and endless adaptations of means to ends in arranging the numerous halls and chambers and staircases for a perfectly domestic purpose, whilst the character of a fortress is not forgotten, afford many an interesting study for a modern architect accustomed to make his plans with far simpler and fewer ideas in view.

AN ENGLISH KING. 29

whilst the usual crowd of human onlookers of a feudal hall was exchanged for the multitudes of goats which then, as now, clustered on the neighbouring crags and rocks inspecting their visitors with the solemn curiosity of their yellow eyes.

On the 17th September the king and his party proceeded on the way southwards to regain the coast after this little tour into the interior of the newly constituted Norman principality. They followed the great road from Naples to Reggio, by way of Potenza and the Val di Diano. Many famous old cities and towns were passed en route, which have since those days completely disappeared in consequence of the constant earthquakes which periodically wreck southern Italy. King Richard must have seen the mediæval city of Potenza in all the importance of its earlier existence ; he would not recognize it at the present day in the few ruins which survive after the earthquake of 1857 when 30,000 persons perished within its walls.

No high road in Italy abounds in more magnificent scenery than that which the English king traversed towards Calabria. The valley of Diano is the centre of the classical Lucania, and here the singular survival of the Hellenic character of the natives was sufficiently evident in the twelfth century. Greek names of places, a Greek idiom or dialect, and the survival of innumerable manners and customs inherent in the Byzantine Empire, gave to the English party of travellers their first impressions of the Levantines or " Griffons " as they were called, with whom they would have soon so much to do both as enemies and as friends.

But perhaps the greatest singularity in the country, at least to English eyes, was the evidence everywhere of its being permanently occupied by two nationalities sufficiently distinct. The villagers and farmers, and to a great extent the bourgeoisie of the towns were of Græco-Roman origin, with their diminutive stature, their swarthy skins, and dark hair and eyes ; the dwellers in the numerous newly built castles, and all the men who occupied the positions of government employees or magistrates were as evidently of northern race with tall figures, and blue eyes and flaxen hair. The contrast presented by these two distinct types was forced upon the attention by the fact that as yet that fusion and amalgamation into what we now call the Neapolitans, showed but little prospect of taking place ; it took seven centuries of endless change and revolution in the kingdom of the two Sicilies to effect the birth of a new nation. The Anglo-Norman king may perhaps have drawn a comparison between the political conditions of Calabria and his own realms, but for a century and a quarter the fusion of Norman and Saxon had been rapidly proceeding in England, and the two races being both of northern origin their mutual affinities were naturally greater than would be found between Norman and Greek.

From the beautiful valley of the Diano the road led by the picturesque Lagonegro down to the seashore at Scalea, a quaintly built town on terraces, surmounted by a Norman castle ; then on to Cetraro, a small town on a high hill overhanging the sea, where in those days there was a priory of the Benedictines of Monte Cassino, at which the king lodged for the night of the 19th September. This priory was known as St. Michael de Iosophat, and a few miles farther along the coast at a place called St. Lucido, was another priory of the same Order, called St. Maria de Fosses, here also the king spent some time.

A strange mingling of classic traditions, half understood, and of perverted mediæval legends, imparted a sense of the unreal and the mysterious to every landmark and natural feature of the scenery in those days of a simple child-like faith and confidence. Whilst lingering on the beautiful southern shores of the Tyrrhene Sea Richard was shown many a site of fabulous or marvellous events, or associated with names distinguished in past history— places which have long since faded from popular recognition, or been superseded by more modern traditions. Near the sea coast he was taken to see the " Study " of Lucan the famous poet who committed suicide to escape the death which Nero threatened him with, out of jealousy of his genius. This underground chamber was probably some imposing Roman or Etruscan tomb which had received such an appellation : its roof supported by massive stone piers, its walls decorated with paintings, the whole more suggestive to the northern visitor of a magnificent apartment for the living, than a tomb for the dead.

On the 20th September Richard journeyed on to the small ancient town of Amantea, where relics of a classic

AN ENGLISH KING. 31

age were scattered around, and near by he had to cross the famous stream of the Busento, where even at the present day the untouched tomb of the Goth Alaric may still be hidden beneath a watery veil. Here, in the bed of the stream, says Gibbon, " the ferocious character of the barbarians was displayed in the funeral of a hero whose valour and fortune they celebrated with mournful applause. By the labour of a captive multitude they forcibly diverted the course of the Busentinus. The royal sepulchre, adorned with the spoils and trophies of Rome was constructed in the vacant bed; the waters were then restored to their natural channels, and the secret spot where the remains of Alaric had been deposited was for ever concealed by the inhuman massacre of the prisoners who had been employed to execute the work." This would be one of the local traditions recounted to interest the stranger king on his way through this land where Goth and Greek were being welded together under Norman influence.

The road pursued by the English king and his retainers led to the then flourishing city of Mileto, capital of the Calabrian peninsula. A world of olive-groves spread out its charms before their eyes, but the orange tree was not so prominent a feature in the landscape as in modern days. Feathery palms and grey rocks offered a contrast to the soft foliage of the olive and the vine, and here and there a small village or a house peering through the vegetation enhanced the attractions of a beautiful prospect. Far off in the direction of their journey sparkled the white town of Scylla on the sea coast, whilst the majestic outline of Etna, with its snowy crest and plume of smoke could be dimly defined on the extreme horizon.

From the road followed by the king's party, not only was Etna sighted, but across the wide expanse of sea visible from the higher levels of the path, the still stranger and more weird apparition of the burning island of Stromboli rose into view.

To the mediæval imagination, volcanoes were the evident entrances into the infernal regions, of the existence of which they were moreover a sufficient demonstration. Not much more ignorant than we moderns are, of the real nature of these terrific phenomena, they had at least the consolation of being able to explain their existence in a way which satisfied themselves—they were merely the abodes of devils and wicked persons condemned to fiery expiation.

King Richard continued his way through a paradise of flowers, where even the villages are named from their varied scents, and the surrounding mountains are clothed with glorious forests, to the abode of the Sicilian kings—of which, now alas ! not a vestige remains.

The Sicilian bailiff and many Norman knights met the king at a short distance from the city of Mileto, to welcome him and form an escort. The royal cavalcade then entered the city with a fanfare of trumpets and the banners of the two lions of Normandy side by side with the spread eagle of Sicily, and as the last horsemen disappeared beneath the archway of the gate, the heavy doors were swung to, and the drawbridge rose on its rattling chains and great counterpoise beams, sliding back into its place over the doorway ; for it was evening time, and a mediæval fortress was always closed to the outside world between sunset and sunrise.

The King of England was accommodated with all due ceremony in the royal palace, or rather citadel, and on the following morning from a tower, enjoyed a distant view of the Straits of Messina. His tour amongst the Norman principalities of southern Italy was almost ended he would now be obliged to return to the hard work of governing the ill-disciplined forces which owed him allegiance, and the still more onerous task of thwarting the designs of his secret adversaries.

At Mileto, a curiosity, a military engine which, one hundred years old, surviving from the time when Robert Guiscard was besieging his younger brother the "Great Count," in that city, seems to have afforded Richard the idea for the famous wooden moveable tower which he afterwards designed for use at Messina and Acre.[1]

Mileto, favourite residence of Count Roger and his wife Eremberga, possessed the magnificent cathedral of the Holy Trinity, and the great Benedictine Abbey of

---

([1]) Such towers commonly used in mediæval warfare, are claimed to have been invented by Julius Cæsar (*vide* "De bello gallico" Bk. II.) although there are many legends of similar war-engines amongst the ancients of a remote period. In the fourth century B.C. some such machine is said to have been used at the famous siege of Salamis in Cyprus.

AN ENGLISH KING. 33

Santa Eufemia, and within a short distance was the retreat of St. Bruno and his Carthusians. In those days the fortress-like buildings of these Norman monks gave a northern character to the neighbourhood which has since been entirely swept away by endless earthquakes.

King Richard was now about to cross over into the island of Sicily, and his mind was occupied with a difficult problem affecting his youngest sister, Joan Plantagenet, married to William II., third king of Sicily, who had died in 1189, without posterity. Three parties in Sicily contested the vacant throne : an Englishman, Walter Miller, Archbishop of Palermo, sought to secure it for Constance the aunt of William II. ; a second party adhered to the cause of the dowager queen Joan, whilst a third under Matteo d'Agello commonly called the "Kaid" had succeeded in having an illegitimate son of Roger, II. named Tancred crowned at Palermo. This last faction represented a Greek or Saracen element in the people—a kind of nationalist party opposed to Norman and northern ideas.

The question of the dowager queen's succession to the crown does not appear to have occupied so much the attention of her brother as the more important consideration of an adequate dowry to which she was entitled, and her claims to certain treasures devised to her by her late husband. When once these matters had been settled we hear no more of her claims upon the Sicilian kingdom.

The curious termination of Richard Cœur de Lion's travels in southern Italy is mentioned only in the chronicle of Roger of Hoveden : neither Richard of Devizes, nor Geoffrey de Vinsauf refer to it.

De Hoveden, a famous lawyer and one of the court historians of the time, whom Green in his history of the English people praises as an accurate and well informed chronicler, states that King Richard departed from Mileto for the Straits of Messina, with a single knight as his attendant or squire. His reason for this proceeding would doubtless have been to escape the tedious ceremonials of departure, and still more the elaborate and possibly embarrassing state reception which awaited him in Sicily. He may also have had some ulterior motive in wishing thus to arrive incognito—the princes of that age were very fond of discovering the state of public opinion or politics in such a way, when as yet the printed news-sheet with its more or less mendacious reports had not been invented for the purpose of obviating the necessity of such investigations.

The high road from Mileto as in the days of King Richard still leads downwards to the once populous town of Gioja on the sea coast although since his time the terrific earthquake of 1783 has destroyed every trace of the Norman abbeys and castles which had been built amongst the chestnut forests and olive groves of the country side. The centre of the awful convulsion of nature was in fact amongst the villages with Greek names which cluster on the higher ground of this part of the coast. Here the king was passing through " a certain small town " (probably Gioja) when he observed in a house on its outskirts the cry of a hawk. With the instinct of a sportsman—to the mediæval knight hawking was the keenest of all sports—he was irresistibly attracted to the place, and entered, to find a very fine bird which he immediately longed to possess.

But unfortunately the owner of the hawk was not disposed to part with it, whereat the king proceeded to act in a somewhat felonious manner forgetful of his royal dignity, and without more ado mounted the bird on his fist and prepared to leave the house. This summary proceeding was resisted by the people of the house, and on his refusing to give up the bird, they summoned their neighbours who came running together from every quarter, armed with sticks and stones with which they attacked the two stranger knights.

Such a grotesque scene seems somewhat incredible, the King of England *en flagrant délit* with a stolen hawk on his wrist in the midst of a group of angry peasants—it reminds one perhaps of a story by Boccacio, or of the pages of Don Quixote. The king must have felt sure of his incognito, and was equally certain of his ability to overcome the peasants—but an accident upset his reckoning. The owner of the hawk and his friends were determined not to submit to such barefaced robbery ; we can easily imagine the clamour, the shrieks of the women, the barking of dogs, the exclamations in different languages, and also the haughty demeanour of the two strangers—but amongst the villagers there was probably

AN ENGLISH KING. 35

Sicilian blood if not Norman, ready to resist aggression even on the part of lordly crusaders armed and clad in mail. One of the peasants drew a great knife and made a determined attack on the king, who in his turn unsheathed his sword and struck at the peasant with the flat of it— it was dishonourable to shed peasant blood although one might steal his property! But—" Dex aie " as the king no doubt said to himself—there was a flaw in the steel, it broke in half! With the stump of his sword he managed to ward off his assailant, and then the two knights disguised, with some difficulty managed to defend themselves with stones, and beat a hasty retreat. Presumably the hawk was left behind!

Making good their escape from the enraged " contadini," King Richard and his companion proceeded on their way to the monastery of Bagnara, about five miles from the Faro, or mouth of the Straits of Messina, here they passed the night, and the following morning crossed over to Sicily still disguised as knights-errant. The king passed his first night on Sicilian soil in a tent at the base of a ruined tower at the Faro.

The "Arbalète à tour" of the twelfth and thirteenth centuries, equivalent of the modern "field-gun," used for shooting "Greek fire," hot iron, and various projectiles.

CHAPTER IV.

THE Straits of Messina presented a busy scene at the end of the year 1191. Crowds of English and French transports and merchant vessels lay at anchor, and on both shores were camps filled with knights and their retainers; it was both impressive and inspiring. But such an army, camped amongst alien surroundings, without adequate discipline and surrounded by disreputable camp-followers, was liable to disorders. A woman selling bread had attacked a man with violence and insults, scratching his face and tearing his hair, because he refused to pay what she demanded. This had led to a faction fight between the soldiery and the citizens of Messina. Ill-will and the natural antagonism between such different types of humanity as Arabs, Greeks, and Normans was springing up or becoming intensified.[1]

The city of Messina was one of the richest commercial communities of the period. Its citizens were chiefly "Lombards," *i.e.* of the half German race of the north of Italy, whose ancestors had migrated during the Dark Ages to the south. A proud conceited society of opulent burghers who thought themselves strong enough within their walls and towers to defy the Crusaders, as a mere

[1] Vinsauf, II. 15.

AN ENGLISH KING. 37

troop of ragged marauders to be kept at a distance. With the unamiable policy of setting one half of the Crusaders against the others, they endeavoured to gain over the apathetic King of France.

The King of England hearing, on his arrival, of the insults which his people had received from the Messinesi, summoned a conference, in the midst of which a cry was raised that Anglo-Normans were being slain by the burghers. The king hurrying to the spot endeavoured to calm the commotion by his presence and fair words, but was received with threats and revilings: on this he and his people withdrew outside the city, the trumpets meanwhile sounding "to arms!"

The townspeople suddenly sobered on finding their folly had brought upon them a well merited reprisal, appealed to the French for help: but with little avail. The walls, the catapults, and engines of defence for a beleagured town, were then manned by the garrison said to be 50,000 available citizens.

In making a reconnaissance of the fortifications on the day of the attack, King Richard had observed a small postern which was feebly barricaded with planks and old timber. Saying nothing the king noted it well, and the following night whilst the attention of the besieged was diverted by a general attack, Richard with two chosen companions, under cover of the darkness, waded across the moat to the little gateway, and with considerable labour succeeded in breaking through the barricade with hatchets. Whilst they were thus engaged a general assault was taking place, and the English ships were breaking the chain of the harbour-mouth in spite of the French who were lodged in the port quarter of the town, and made some pretence to defend it.

At the end of more than an hour the two strong men who were assisting King Richard were whispering that a passage had been made through the splintered timber and rubbish. One of them crawled through into the small chamber within, and the king ever anxious to be first, quickly followed. With care and in silence the three Normans found themselves within the city, and apparently unobserved. For a moment they listened to the cries of defiance, and the shouts of the besiegers and besieged on the other sides of the fortress, and could see the flare lights and the pots of Greek-fire flying through the night-darkness from the slings and trebuchets like modern rockets. But this was a momentary pause, King Richard immediately set about finding the inside of the city gate which was the object in view.[1]

Gliding along the inside of the curtain, and unnoticed in its shadow by the guards on its summit engaged in observing the movements of the besiegers across the moat, the three companions in this hazardous adventure succeeded in reaching the inside of the city gate. Here fortune favoured them in a marvellous manner. The inside of the gate was unguarded!

The men-at-arms had been sent elsewhere, and the sentinels and warders were in the upper storey of the tower above the gate. Quick as lightning the three adventurers saw and seized their opportunity: they immediately unfastened the counterpoise beams of the drawbridge, which descended into its place across the moat. At the same time they slid the great beam forming the wooden bolt at the back of the gate into its long chase in the wall at the side of the entrance, and by good fortune the portcullis not having been lowered they were able to undo the other fastenings of the door with a few blows of their hatchets.

As Richard and his two assistants threw open the gate, a party of his men rushed in across the drawbridge: the entrance was secured, and the city was won, and by the time the garrison had realized these happenings it was too late to offer any resistance. Messina had been taken by a cleverly planned assault, which suited the genius of the best military engineer of his time, as Cœur de Lion certainly proved himself to be.

Scenes of bloodshed and rapine, murder and pillage, quickly followed on the capture of the city, such as must always occur when the desperate and terrified inhabitants attempt to resist the rude onslaught of an undisciplined soldiery. Whilst the city was being given up to plunder, many of the Messinesi retired to the upper floors of their houses, and continued to harass the invaders with stones and arrows, with the inevitable result of prolonging and intensifying the conflict. Meanwhile King Richard made such efforts as were possible to mitigate the horrors of the struggle.[2]

[1] **Vinsauf II., 16.**   [2] Ibid. II., 16.

AN ENGLISH KING. 39

The dawn of the first of October revealed the condition of a mediæval city which had been plundered and subdued by force during the dark hours of night. In some few places houses had been set on fire, and were still burning. Everywhere were traces of disorder and street fighting, and many stark forms of dead men lay about the roads or in corners where the wounded had crawled out of the way of the combatants. Men-at-arms wandered about laden with spoil from the houses which had been looted, and from whence sounds of revelry came showing that many of the plunderers were drowning their feelings of animosity towards their enemies in deep potations of enemy liquor. The capturing of prisoners and an effort to bring the citizens who still showed some spirit of resistance, within a necessary control, occupied the attention of Anglo-Norman sergeants and knights appointed to the charge of the conquered city.

The conquest of Messina had been rapidly accomplished —in as little time as a priest would chant mattins, according to one chronicler—but the operations had been complicated by the presence of the French king resident for the time being within its walls. The French now demanded that the city should be placed under a dual control, a demand conceded by King Richard with some demur, and the banners of France and Normandy were then placed side by side upon the towers.[1]

King Richard who was encamped upon a hill near by the city, now built a wooden tower, probably on rollers, or " Beffroi," such as was used in attacking a fortress, which could be moved against the walls in such a way as to render their defence hopeless. This tower, called " Mategriffon " was so ingeniously constructed as to admit of being taken to pieces and transported in the fleet for later use at Acre. The appearance of this moveable tower caused the " Griffons " of Messina the greatest alarm, and its moral effect was even more important upon King Tancred, who, shortly after its construction, sent an embassy to King Richard to express the most profound apologies for the people of Messina, and the assurance of his perfect friendship and goodwill. In addition, the embassy brought to King Richard 40,000 ounces of gold, in payment of Queen Joan's dowry.[2]

[1] Vinsauf II., 17.   [2] Richard of Devizes, secs. 27. 28.

Tancred's unexpected liberality aroused a corresponding generosity in the mind of King Richard, and the largesse which he distributed amongst the Crusaders, and through them to the tradesmen of Messina did much towards smoothing over the traces of recent troubles. The King of France was also induced out of rivalry to imitate the English king's liberality.

The "Mategriffon" of Richard Cœur de Lion.
[Conjectural restoration.]

Archbishop Walter of Rouen who had taken the Cross, but afterwards changed his mind, induced many of the knights and soldiers to restore the property which they had looted in Messina. He induced the English king to do so, and those who did not follow such an example were visited with anathema and excommunication—important penalties in those days.

But alas! in the general pacification of affairs, some Genoese and Pisan sailors who had drunk themselves

AN ENGLISH KING. 41

into a quarrelsome mood nearly succeeded in setting everyone at loggerheads again. Attacking the crews of English ships moored at the quay, several men were killed on either side, and King Richard who was quickly on the spot only separated the combatants with difficulty.

The knights who had been at great expense for a long time awaiting the departure of the two kings for the Levant, received the largesse of King Richard as a sort of compensation for their restitution of the loot taken at Messina ; many widows and orphans who had found their way from the Holy Land to Sicily were also supported on the king's bounty.

King Tancred, who resided at Palermo, was desirous of meeting the King of England, and it was decided that the interview should take place at a small town named Cefalù, midway between Messina and Palermo. Here the two monarchs made acquaintance and as was customary in those days were first conducted into the cathedral to hear mass as part of the ceremonial interview. The newly built cathedral was still in the hands of the mosaic artists, but the colossal figures of saints and angels which we still see in the dim obscurity of its singularly lofty interior, were perhaps almost as impressive then, as they seem to us now, stretching hands of benediction out of golden skies, as they did seven hundred years ago over the heads of the kings of Sicily and England.[1]

The visit of King Richard to King Tancred at Cefalù had taken place at the end of the year 1190, but it had been so timed as to admit of Cœur de Lion's return to Messina for the holding of his Christmas feast—in other words he was able to "keep his Christmas" amongst his own people at "Mategriffon."[2]

The Christmas feast of the twelfth century had a character and importance peculiar to the period, it was, as it perhaps still is amongst northern races, the principal feast of the year—the turning point of the winter solstice, when the sun once more renews its power amongst the fogs and clouds of a northern latitude—the Yule-tide of the Normans.

[1] Vinsauf II., 22. Cefalu is intended although the name given for the town is "Fatina."
[2] Ibid. II., 24.

The three masses of Christmas Eve, 1190, were duly observed in the Crusaders camp. The kings with their courts of nobles and knights, assisted at the " cockcrow " celebrations by the archbishops and bishops in the different royal chapels, which had been formed for the purpose, and on the following morning after some repose the great festival of the year was inaugurated with a suitable outburst of trumpets and military music. The Zampognari of the Abruzzi were also on the spot, to add their bagpipes and shrill pandean pipes to the cheerful sounds of an awaking encampment.

A few days previously King Richard had invited, with all respect, the King of France to the feast which he proposed making at " Mategriffon," and this courteous invitation had been accepted. Then the King of England had by a public crier, called on all the Crusaders to join with him in observing Christmas Day with joy and feasting.

The feast prepared by King Richard was to take place at midday and occupy the greater part of the afternoon. The open space within the stoccade of " Mategriffon " was arranged with suitable tents and awnings, and the tables as usual formed a hollow square, one side of which consisted of the " higher tables " for the two kings and the greater nobles.

At the hour appointed, the clamour resounding in the neighbourhood of " Mategriffon," incident to the crowd of cooks and scullions preparing the food, was overpowered by the more blatant and continuous notes of the trumpeters announcing the arrival of the French king and his court. The King of England and his courtiers were already stationed within the enclosure, the king seated on a faldstool, or folding throne. At the entrance of Philip, the English king rose to welcome him, and the two kings embraced each other with the traditional kiss of peace. Then the King of England led his royal brother to the high table which had been prepared for them on a dais beneath a richly embroidered canopy, and the two kings having seated themselves, the attendant courtiers did likewise in their appointed places, and according to their several degrees. The horns were then sounded for the " corner l'eau," at which the assembled company dipped their fingers in basins of water presented by kneeling varlets.

AN ENGLISH KING. 43

The culinary art of southern Italy has always been famous for its variety and richness—maceheroni and gnocchi, served in a dozen different ways, the delicious sword-fish and tunny, wild boar and venison, augmented the ordinary mutton or goat and swine flesh of the period, and afforded some surprise for the northern pilgrims.

Behind the convives stood varlets ready to keep their cups filled with the famous white wine of Sicily, at that time the most delicate table wine in the world.[1]

Between the courses and their tedious service and the tasting by the proper officials, the ceremonial presentation, and the eventual placing of the meats on their *tranchèes* of bread before each noble seigneur, a space was cleared in the centre of the enclosure, on which a number of players or mummers enacted a representation of the "Adoration of the Magi," as being appropriate to the season.

At the conclusion of the repast, after the cloths and napkins had been removed, and sweetmeats and wine placed before the guests, the King of England caused several gold cups of the richest and most varied designs to be presented to Philip Augustus, for him to select a gift from in honour of the occasion. He also gave to each of the nobles a token of remembrance in accordance with his rank.

According to Master Geoffrey's record of this feast, the display of gold and silver cups and platters was astonishing. Many of them were decorated with figures of men and animals of finest workmanship—possibly in the style of the Damascus brass cups so popular as finger bowls at the present day. Many of them were incrusted with precious stones, in the same way as the cups looted by the crusaders at Constantinople in 1204, which still lie in the treasury of St. Mark at Venice.

The departure of the King of France from the banquet was accompanied by the same ceremonial as at his arrival. The trumpeters sounded their clarions and horns, and the procession of nobles formed a guard of honour around the two kings as far as the gate of the stoccade. Here the same ceremonial of embracing was performed and both kings having now retired from the scene, their retainers and guests were left to continue their conviviality until a later hour.[2]

[1] Viollet le Duc.   [2] Vinsauf II., 24.

At length the season for navigation and seafaring drew on ; the winter with its tempests was past, and the people hailed with joy the prospect of departure from Messina. To those of the Crusaders gifted with foresight the long delay seemed a singularly unfortunate beginning to the expedition. Six months had been wasted in idleness and all the evils attendant on idleness, treasure and resources had been frittered away, debts and bad habits had been the only results in this enervating climate amongst a rabble of the worst camp-followers, whilst the news from Acre brought by refugees was most disquieting. How many of the Crusaders must have been inclined to turn back, and indeed it proved very difficult for the leaders to keep their followers together, the desertions were of daily occurrence and the pledges given were often abandoned.[1]

The festival of the Annunciation of the Blessed Virgin Mary in 1191, (March 25th) became memorable as the date when the long delayed Third Crusade at last began to leave the Straits of Messina. The King of France had pressed on the equipment of his transports and big ships, and on the Saturday following the festival, the fleet put out to sea, steering for Cape Spartavento, and the long six months encampment of the French was at an end (30th March, Mas Latrie).

The eastern Mediterranean lay basking in the sunshine of early spring, its rippling wavelets recalled the Homeric simile of " Old Ocean's myriad smile," and all seemed propitious for a prosperous voyage. As an act of courtesy to his ally and suzerain King Richard ordered out some Anglo-Norman galleys to accompany the French fleet for a short distance on its way eastwards, and occupied one of them himself, in order to bid farewell to his brother monarch where the mighty form of Etna rises from the waters as the most stupendous sea-mark in the world.

Hurrying back from this short voyage King Richard's galley was steered for Reggio, where his mother the dowager-queen Eleanor had just arrived, escorting his betrothed, the Princess Berengaria, daughter of Sancho VI. King of Navarre. These ladies, attended by an imposing body of men-at-arms and retainers had journeyed along the Riviera and down the Italian coast. At Pisa they had

[1] Vinsauf II., 23, and Richard of Devizes, sec. 33.

AN ENGLISH KING. 45

passed some time awaiting news from the camp at Messina ; then the arrangements having been concluded for the departure of the army they had arrived just in time for the Princess Berengaria to proceed in the English fleet, on the understanding that her marriage to the King of England would take place on arrival in the Holy Land.[1]

The family affairs of the Plantagenets had been the reverse of happy or fortunate. The father and mother of Richard Cœur de Lion were both regarded by their contemporaries as wanting in moral character. Henry II's. illegitimate family by Rosamund Clifford, not to mention numerous other claimants to his royal parentage, suggest a comparison with Charles II. His amours with the betrothed bride of his son Cœur de Lion (the Princess Alice of France) were probably the very justifiable cause of the estrangement between him and his successor on the English throne, and in any case showed a singular weakness of character. Under the circumstances the relations between Henry and his legitimate wife Eleanor must have been sufficiently stormy, and reached their climax when the queen was imprisoned for no less a period than ten years on a charge of murdering Rosamund Clifford.

Eleanor of Acquitaine, Queen of England, was a woman of headstrong will and a remarkable physique. In her youth she had been married to Louis VII., King of France, and had accompanied him on the Second Crusade, at the head of a sort of amazonian contingent. Riding or carried in a litter with the crusading armies and their lumbering baggage trains through what is now Servia, she was accustomed to all the wild and savage scenes of a mediæval army on the march : the armed men surrounded by an undisciplined rabble of pilgrims and followers, the drunkenness and profligacy and also the religious fanaticism. From a terrible battle at Laodicea in Asia Minor, she and her youthful husband escaped to Adalia, and from thence journeyed by sea to Antioch.

A picturesque legend is told of Eleanor's arrival at Jerusalem in 1149. On entering the church of the Holy Sepulchre with her husband Louis VII., and a crowd of noble courtiers, the Holy Sites were visited in the customary order, although the greater part of them was covered

[1] Mas Latrie "Histoire de l'ile de Chypre," I., 2.

by still unfinished buildings. As the royal party approached the entrance into the church from the Patriarchate, a ragged hermit who had taken up his residence in a dark corner—appropriately called in those days by the suggestive title of an "in pace"—suddenly started out in front of the queen, wildly denouncing her for certain conduct at Antioch, and for her intrigues with her uncle the Prince of Antioch, and even with certain Saracen emirs. He also accused her of a general responsibility in the deplorable failure of the Second Crusade. As if this were not enough the apparition concluded his fierce harangue by claiming her as his daughter, to the speechless astonishment of the bystanders. Such a claim however proved to be supported by the fact that this ragged unrecognizable fakir was no less a personage than William VIII. Count of Poitou and Guienne, who some years before had retired to live a life of voluntary penance in Jerusalem.

It is not recorded what the relations of the father and daughter so strangely brought together in the Holy Sepulchre church may have subsequently been, but the Count of Poitou did not remain for long in the Holy City, preferring to retire to a desert *sierra* in Spain, where he was able to ensure a still greater tranquillity than Jerusalem appears to have afforded him, and there he finished his existence in solitude and oblivion.

Louis VII. and Eleanor of Acquitaine returned to France after Easter, 1149, and in 1152 their divorce took place by mutual consent, and with the sanction of the Pope : consanguinity, that simple and easy excuse for separating married folk in the middle ages being alleged. Within a few months, Eleanor as Duchess of Acquitaine, Auvergne, Poitou, and Guienne, married Henry II. King of England, Duke of Anjou, Maine and Normandy.

Eleanor, in the course of a very long life—after reigning as queen in both France and England—was to see three of her sons crowned in succession as kings of England, and of an English dominion which in those days extended over the whole of England, half Ireland, and the greater half of what we now call France. She had seen Jerusalem when the Latin Kingdom of the Levant was at its zenith, and now in its dissolution when her third son Richard

AN ENGLISH KING. 47

was attempting its rescue. At the time of her arrival at Reggio, as the duenna of her son's affianced bride Berengaria, the Dowager Queen of England must have been sixty-seven years old, but still full of vigour and energy. The royal galley was no sooner moored in Reggio harbour than King Richard hurrying ashore to the lodging of his mother, was able to salute her and his betrothed with due expressions of joy and welcome. With the ladies were the ambassadors from the King of Navarre, and other officers attached to the household of the princess. The poop of the galley having been prepared with its awnings for the reception of the ladies, they were received on board with the usual demonstrations by a crowd of the townspeople collected at the quayside, whilst musicians on the fo'castle sounded their instruments. Then setting sail the royal party arrived at Messina in a couple of hours, and there for more than a fortnight the queen-mother, her son and daughter and her future daughter-in-law held their family councils.

The circumstances of King Richard's betrothal to the daughter of the King of Navarre are imperfectly recorded. In his youth he had been affianced to Adela (or Alice) daughter of Louis VII. and sister of Philip II. of France, and this engagement held good until the death of Henry II., who for some years had acted as the guardian of the French princess. On inheriting the crown of England Richard broke off this promise of marriage, and this had much to do with the unsatisfactory position of affairs between the kings of France and England during the Third Crusade. According to Richard of Devizes, King Richard consulted the astute and treacherous Philip, Count of Flanders, "who possessed an invaluable power of speech." The count's mediation resulted in Philip, King of France releasing Richard from his engagement on payment of 10,000 pounds of silver, together with the surrender of the border territory between France and Normandy, known as the Vexin, with its castle of Gisors. This transaction was not without its humiliations on both sides, as so often occurs in breach of promise cases, and if Richard lost his money, the French king and his sister became the objects of much scandalous criticism.

Queen Eleanor had also to do with this matter. Evidently her policy was adverse to the French king, the son of her first husband by a second wife, and she is credited with bringing about the marriage with Berengaria. Under the circumstances she doubtless found it convenient to delay her journey down the Italian coast, until the moment of the French king's departure from Messina, as her journey had been undertaken for the purpose of concluding the contract between her son and the princess whom she had chosen for his wife. Her arrival had been carefully timed for the purpose at Reggio, and she was in time to witness the passing out of the straits of the French fleet with Philip II., the Duke of Burgundy, the Count Philip of Flanders, and many a French knight and lord of high degree on board, their flags and pennons floating in the wind, whilst the sounds of music were borne across the waves to the spectators on either shore.

AN ENGLISH KING.   49

Crossbow.

CHAPTER V.

THE final preparations for the departure of the Anglo-Normans drew on apace, for the King of England and his followers were naturally as impatient of the delay which had taken place, and anxious to leave Messina as their French allies had been. The provisioning of their ships was therefore hurried on, and also the infinitude of details which the conveyance of an army of men and horses by sea must always involve. In addition to the baggage and foodstuffs, we hear for the first time of the movable siege machinery—the artillery of the period—being stowed away on board ship. The wonderful " Mategriffon " was taken to pieces, and packed up for future use in the siege of Acre. Catapults, trebuchets, and such-like machines were now constructed in such a way as to be easily packed for transport, and such things were beginning to be used to a certain extent on board ship. Whilst these laborious operations were in progress, King Richard and his council were discussing the regency of his dominions during his absence from Europe.

Walter, Archbishop of Rouen, who had been very instrumental in pacifying Sicily after the siege of Messina by the English, and had even secured the return of much loot to the citizens of the plundered town was now allowed to return to his diocese, but not without paying a heavy fine for changing his mind and abandoning the Crusade.

The Holy Week of the year 1191 was the period chosen for the departure of the Anglo-Normans from the Straits of Messina. On Palm Sunday after mass in the cathedral and with all due ceremonial of benediction and augury for a prosperous voyage, the Princess Berengaria with her attendant companion the Dowager Queen of Sicily, was conducted on board one of the largest dromons of the fleet. This vessel carrying three masts, and of about the size and tonnage of a small modern frigate, was not propelled by oars, and was consequently not expected to arrive in Acre before the rest of the fleet, even with the advantage of a few days' start. Several trusted knights and a retinue of servants had been accommodated on board, so that every preparation had been made for the comfort and guardianship of the two princesses. With the midday breeze blowing down the straits from the north, the dromon was hauled up to her anchors, and the great sails began to fill as she was brought round on the eastern course heading for the Ægean sea. With streamers flying and the armories of Navarre and Sicily displayed on her high poop, and with the usual accompaniment of music in the fo'castle, the ship passed beyond Cape Spartavento and in a few hours was lost to view.

With the departure of his future bride, the undivided attention of King Richard was given to the manœuvring of the main fleet and its orderly arrangement. Possibly for the first time in English history the presence of a High Admiral of the navy is recorded in the person of Robert de Torneham, or Turnham, who received on this occasion the commission to conduct and take care of the fleet. This seigneur must have been a relative, if not a brother, of King Richard's favourite steward during the campaign in Palestine, often mentioned under the name of Stephen de Torneham in the chronicles.

A review of the fleet was necessary before the actual sailing took place, and the Straits of Messina presented a sight on the Tuesday after Palm Sunday which has seldom been seen before or since within their narrow limits. For this purpose the ships of the Anglo-Norman, or English fleet, were marshalled in six lines not far from the shore, in such a way that they could be easily inspected by the king in his row-boat or small galley. In the outer line were ranged the busses and dromons to the number of thirteen; in the next row were fourteen similar ships, and in the third, twenty; in the fourth, thirty, and in the fifth, forty; in the sixth row nearest the shore were more

AN ENGLISH KING.   51

than sixty smaller ships or galleys. The larger ships and transports numbered about seventy, and the total of all sizes amounted to more than one hundred and fifty. Such a fleet was sufficiently important in spite of the fact that many of the ships would be regarded as very small compared with the war-vessels of later times. The ships were arranged at such distances from each other that the sound of the human voice could be heard between each vessel in a line, whilst the notes of the trumpet could be used for conveying orders between the lines.[1]

Richard of Devizes states that about one hundred and fifty ships took part in the above mentioned review, but he also mentions in another place that the grand total of King Richard's fleet amounted to two hundred and nineteen.

Benedict of Peterboro' states the departure to have taken place on 10th April, 1191, and the fleet to have consisted of one hundred and fifty large ships and fifty-three smaller ones or galleys.

The review or muster having taken place, the king entertained certain Sicilian dignitaries at a grand banquet on shore; here with the usual diplomatic expressions of regret at leaving the hospitable shores of Sicily, the king and his army took leave in a formal manner of a place where so many episodes of a disagreeable character had occurred.

On that Tuesday afternoon in Holy Week, 1191, King Richard stepped on board his galley, and within an hour the whole fleet which was in waiting had drawn up their moorings and was in movement on an eastern course with the mighty sea-mark of Etna on the starboard bow.

At the head of the fleet sailed the royal galley, with oars supplementing the great lateen sails of its two masts. On its main mast the red cross banner fluttered in the breeze during daylight, to be replaced as night closed in with a lantern, containing a wax candle, intended to be the guiding light for the whole fleet. The ships proceeded on their due course and in perfect order until past Cape Spartavento, and the mouth of the Adriatic sea was reached, here, as often occurs, the weather changed, and a storm was brewing.

[1] Richard of Devizes, sec. 59.

Off the coast of Calabria a dead calm prevailed, continuing all the day following the departure from the straits; on the morrow, that is to say Holy Thursday, a northwest wind sprang up which carried the ships on their course until the morning of Good Friday, when the impending storm broke and increased until the crews and passengers were alike filled with terror—those of them, that is to say, who were not too overcome with sea-sickness to be almost insensible to the roar of the tempest, the dashing of the waves, and the evident helplessness of the sailors and their shipmasters. The ships began to part company, and although King Richard, who had ordered his galley to be turned astern in order to collect together the fleet, as far as possible, and did all in his power to animate those who were filled with despair, the consequences might have been disastrous but for a sudden change in the wind, as often takes place in that sea. During the night succeeding this tempestuous Good Friday the weather moderated, and with the great lantern at the masthead of the king's galley leading the way, the greater part of the ships held on their course.

Holy Saturday, the festival of Easter Day, and the Monday and Tuesday following, were spent by the Crusaders on their ships at sea. Each ship above the size of a galley carried a permanent altar on board, placed on the main deck between the two entrances into the cabin of the poop, so that the crucifix above it was attached to the railing of the quarter-deck, or poop. This mediæval custom of carrying a permanent altar on board a ship of any size, is supposed to have been the origin of a custom surviving into comparatively modern times for the sailors on a ship of war to salute when passing before the place on the deck once occupied by the altar.

The offices appropriate to the Easter festival were of course celebrated with all due ceremony and ritual, there being a vast number of clerics of all degrees from archbishops downwards on the several ships. Processions were conducted around the ships' masts in place of the columns of a terrestrial church, and the Blessed Sacrament was exposed for veneration in a tabernacle, or monstrance, very much as if the rites of the church were being performed within the massive fabric of some Norman cathedral instead of in a number of small frail vessels, surrounded

AN ENGLISH KING. 53

by the waves of the eastern Mediterranean, and a boundless horizon.

On Wednesday after Easter the whole fleet came in sight of the island of Crete, where they cruised along the north coast until coming to the natural harbour of Suda Bay, they were able to collect together and land for water and fresh provisions. Here King Richard held a muster of the ships and it was found that twenty-five were missing, much to his grief.

On the following day, Thursday, the king and all his army went on board the ships and put out into the Ægean sea, the wind being very favourable for their course, but towards evening it grew into a gale which impelled the ships violently towards the island of Rhodes. As the dawn of Friday broke, the rocky shores of the island appeared through the surf which lined them, and filled those on board with alarm. However, by turning to the north-west, they made the sheltered port of the city of Rhodes, which still survived from ancient times, although but little used in the twelfth century as a " scala " or place of European commerce. Sixty years before the advent of the Anglo-Normans within its harbours, Rhodes had been plundered and ruined by Venetians, and although there was no openly declared warfare between the Crusaders of 1191 and the Byzantine Empire, the islanders of the Dodecanesia Archipelago very naturally regarded the King of England and his Norman followers as little better than enemies. They however had to put up with the unwelcome presence of this large army for the space of ten days.

Rhodes at the time of King Richard's visit was a mass of ruins, which seems to have reminded the visitors of the city of Rome. Its vast extent, its innumerable towers and ruined houses, its grass-grown streets, and the absence of any population—most of the ordinary residents having fled to the mountains or the mainland on the approach of the Anglo-Normans—impressed the new comers with a sense of its faded grandeur, and made credible the legend of the brazen statue which had once bestridden the entrance to its port. A scarcity of food supplies prevailed, and the foraging expeditions in the island, and on the opposite coasts, revealed the traces of a passed away world and its monuments, such as the Mausoleum of Halicarnassus then still standing to a great extent intact, and the ruins of Cuidus with its colossal lion, which now reposes in the British Museum. In this region, with its legends of the Wonders of the Ancient World, Master Geoffrey the Cellarer found much of interest, and records his thankfulness for a respite from the troubles of shipboard and seafaring whilst studying these ancient remains. During this stay at Rhodes, King Richard fell sick, and this, combined with the necessity for collecting and awaiting the ships which had wandered out of their course or had been lost sight of during the storm of Good Friday, occasioned delay.

It is evident that during the stay of the Crusaders at Rhodes the King of England and his counsellors were entertaining the idea of a conquest of Cyprus. The so-called "Emperor" of Cyprus, Isaac Comnenus, was regarded by everyone as a cruel tyrant whose removal from the scene would benefit not only his unfortunate subjects but also the conditions under which pilgrims and Crusaders were forced to journey towards the Holy Land, in addition to which it was obvious that the possession of the island by Europeans would be of the greatest advantage to the Latin Kingdom of Jerusalem. It is therefore probable that, even if no sufficient excuse had been forthcoming, such as was afterwards provided by the scandalous treatment of shipwrecked crews, and the attempt to capture the ship carrying the princesses at Amathus, an occupation of the island would have been carried out in due course. Such was evidently the opinion of Master Geoffrey.[1]

The voyage of the Crusaders, so much delayed and interrupted, was once more resumed : the reunited fleet, revictualled and in excellent trim set out to cross the Gulf of Adalia, or Sattalia as it was then called. But again the winds were adverse, and a tempest came on which threatened a disaster to the fleet. After much drifting backwards and forwards in contrary winds, the storm abated, and the lookout on the king's ship which was in advance of the others presently spied a stranger vessel on the eastern horizon, which on a nearer approach proved to be a large dromon or buza on her way from Acre to Europe. With alacrity the king ordered a boat to be lowered, and sent enquiries for news on board this ship

[1] Vinsauf, II., 27.

and in this way learnt that the King of France was busy making machines for the siege of Acre, and had already succeeded in beating down part of the walls with petrariœ. This news exhilarated the spirits of the Crusaders, and they passed on their way with joy as the dromon sailing in the opposite direction, fell astern and was quickly lost to sight on the western horizon.

CHAPTER VI.

ON the vigil of St. Mark the Evangelist, towards the end of the month of April, 1191, the coasts of Cyprus were encircled with an ominous line of seething surf. The spirit of the storm was brooding over the troubled waters of the eastern Mediterranean, and dark thunderclouds covered the horizon. Tempestuous winds and mountainous seas had separated the ships of the English fleet, most of them having been obliged to return to Rhodes. Some of the smaller vessels were, however, driven eastwards, and of these three were so unfortunate as to arrive on the rocky western shore of Cyprus in the midst of the gale. Probably due to the ignorance of the shipmasters or their pilots, they ran on shore amongst the rocks instead of making either the port of Papho or the roadstead of Amathus. All three of them became total wrecks, and many of their passengers and crew were drowned. Those who succeeded in getting to shore with the greatest difficulty, found themselves in a wretched plight, having lost money, provisions and clothing.[1]

The arrival of these strangers in the island caused considerable excitement amongst the natives. The villagers of the district at first received them with every expression of goodwill and friendliness, but insisted on their giving up their arms as a sign that they had no hostile intentions towards the country. The new comers were lodged in an old tower, or fortified village near the coast, and within a short time discovered that they were regarded very much as prisoners, awaiting the decision of the despot Isaac Comnenus the then governor of the island, as to their disposal. Notwithstanding this, several of the notables of the island sent them clothing, food, and other necessaries.[2]

Some other ships of the fleet, which had also been driven eastward by the fury of the gale, had successfully weathered its severity, and as it abated, they came to anchor in the roadstead of Amathus. These ships were under the command of Stephen de Turnham the trusty steward and treasurer of Cœur de Lion, who, hearing of the fate of the three wrecked ships, was active in sending

[1] Vinsauf II., 30. [2] Mas Latrie Histoire I., 3.

AN ENGLISH KING. 57

to the survivors of their crews an abundance of provisions, which as it afterwards appeared never reached them. Meanwhile the natives were holding a council at Amathus at which it was determined that the strangers at the village should be kept as prisoners in the place where they then were, and that at a convenient opportunity they should be murdered. This disagreeable decision as to their fate seems to have reached the imprisoned Englishmen, who thereupon decided in spite of being without arms, that it would be wisest to try and break through their enemies and rejoin their friends in the ships at Amathus. They therefore issued from their refuge and approached the port, and on the way were surrounded and attacked by the natives, and several were killed on either side. A certain Roger de Harcourt, having found a horse, mounted it and was able to ride down many of their assailants, and a certain Norman named William Dubois having a bow which he had retained concealed, and being a very dexterous shot, managed to kill many with his arrows.

The men who were on board the ships in Amathus bay having observed the fray which was taking place on shore, immediately divined the cause, and as quickly prepared to assist their comrades. But the natives now showed their hostility and tried to prevent the landing of the Englishmen, so that there were two battles going on in Amathus at the same moment. But a very short time sufficed for the fortune of battle to be decided in favour of the Anglo-Normans. The Cypriots were driven off and the united force of the strangers retired on board their ships to await the expected arrival of the main fleet.

Whilst these events had been taking place on shore a very important addition to the small squadron under the command of Stephen de Turnham in Amathus bay had been made by the arrival of the buza or dromon carrying no less a personage than Berengaria, the bride of Cœur de Lion, and his sister the dowager Queen of Sicily. Being a great ship of the period, and well found, she was fitted to keep the sea, so her shipmaster brought her to an anchorage at some distance from the shore, and as it proved with great advantage to the security of the noble ladies on board.

The hostility of the islanders towards the Crusaders was now manifest, but the same day as the, fracas between the opposing forces took place, the so-called emperor, or more properly speaking, despot of the island, Isaac Comnenus, a relative of the Emperor of Constantinople, arrived on the scene. This man who is accused of all the vices, craft, and cunning which the mediæval chroniclers were in the habit of freely attributing to the Byzantine Greeks, or "Griffons," of the period, appears to have been regarded even by his own people in much the same light. He immediately sought to pacify the angry spirits, and come to terms with the northerners whose reputation for skill and ferocity in warfare had engendered amongst the southern races a terror of their very name. His motives were as much actuated by fear as anything else, and he endeavoured to obtain by duplicity an advantage which he saw would be of the greatest importance in what appeared to be an inevitable struggle. He doubtless felt a foreboding of that new element in the Crusades which was to culminate in the attack upon the whole Byzantine Empire thirteen years later (1204) and of which a preliminary movement would naturally be the occupation of Cyprus by the European allies. With the object in view of coming to terms with the invaders of his country, who already had an excuse for demanding compensation for insults and robberies committed on shipwrecked men, he immediately made offers of every kind of satisfaction, and invited all the newcomers to land and avail themselves of such conveniences and provisions as the island afforded. But he had more especially planned a scheme for entrapping the two royal ladies, whom he desired to secure as hostages against the arrival of the King of England: in this he was foiled, as all his endeavours, accompanied with presents and bland and deceptive messages, met with equally astute and evasive replies and excuses. He endeavoured to persuade the ladies of the much greater security afforded by their coming on land, and he offered to exchange hostages for the due performance of all his promises. But the distrust of a possible enemy was perhaps even greater in those days than at the present; international dislike had not been tempered by humanitarian or philanthropic ideas of modern times. The ship containing the royal bride continued to ride securely at anchor, without any indication that the prize on board would pass into the clutches of the would-be brigands on shore.

AN ENGLISH KING.

The late Dr. Hackett in his most admirable " History of the Church of Cyprus " 1901, has collected together all the facts relating to the life and character of Isaac Comnenus. His authorities are Du Cange " Familiæ Byzantinæ," (1680) Choniates (Patrologia Latina of Migne, CXXXIX.,) Neophytos " De Calamitati Cypri " (1681), and other rare and little-known writers on the period.

Isaac, the last ruler of Greek race in the island, was a somewhat remarkable man. He was the grand-nephew of the Emperor Manuel by whom he was appointed in his youth to be the governor of Tarsus and Cilician Armenia. In this capacity he carried on hostilities with the independent Armenians of the Taurus, and being conquered by them was ransomed from captivity through the exertions of his aunt Theodora, the Dowager Queen of Jerusalem, with a sum of 60,000 bysants drawn from the revenue of Cyprus. The Armenian Prince Rhupen had transferred his captive to the care of the Prince of Antioch, who, receiving half the stipulated ransom, allowed Isaac to proceed to Cyprus to collect the remainder.

On reaching the island the perfidious Isaac showed to the inhabitants forged letters purporting to appoint him the Katapan or governor. No sooner was he firmly established in this position, and had gathered a chosen body of mercenary ruffians around him, than he threw off the mask and openly declared himself to be an independent sovereign with the title of Emperor.

The reigning Emperor of Byzantium, Andronikos, was enraged at the news of this upstart usurping the Cyprian throne, but he was powerless to do more than order the impalement and stoning to death of any friends of Isaac whom he could lay hands on. His anger was mixed with a fear that an old prophecy about his own fall from power through a person whose name should begin with *iota* might come true, but that event was curiously reserved for another Isaac (Angelos) who in 1185, put an end to the bloodstained reign of Andronicos, and himself assumed the purple.

Isaac Comnenus had felt somewhat insecure in his usurpation, he was conscious the empire would endeavour to regain so important a province as Cyprus, and in view of this contingency he had allied himself with William II. King of Sicily, whose sister he married. This alliance was singularly fortunate for him, for in 1186, Isaac Angelos sent an expedition of seventy galleys with a great army to drive the usurper out of the island. But this expedition proved a terrible fiasco for the imperialists. By the greatest good fortune for Comnenus, the famous Sicilian admiral Margaritone, reckoned the greatest seaman of his age, had just finished the successful defence of Tyre against Saladin, and was able to come to the assistance of his Cyprian ally in the most opportune manner. All the Greek galleys were captured at Amathus, and the army which had been landed there also meeting with total defeat, those of the prisoners who refused to enrol themselves in the army of Comnenus were put to death, and the remainder with the chiefs of the expedition were carried off to Palermo.

The admiral Margaritone, in truth a Spaniard, was also related to the Sicilian kings, having married a daughter of William I.

The epoch of the Crusades coincides with the complete decay of the Byzantine Empire. The Comnenian dynasty was its ruin, and with a weak home government such dependencies as Cyprus were easily wrested from the imperial domain by adventurous usurpers. On three occasions, in 1042, 1092, and 1184 Cyprus had become a more or less independent sovereignty, and this independence may have ministered to its eventual absorption into the great feudal system of Europe as a Latin Kingdom. There seems to have been a tendency in the provinces of the Byzantine Empire of the twelfth century to break into subdivisions. The temper of the times was restless and adventurous, and a very perturbing influence was doubtless brought to bear upon the Levantine, as well as the South Italian and Sicilian provinces by the passage of crusading hosts on their way eastward. These Crusaders were frequently hungry northern desperadoes intent upon founding rich and vigorous feudal seigneuries amongst the feeble and degenerating survivors of the once powerful Romaic empire.

The first or greatest of all the Crusades in 1099 had evidently been a result or a development of the marvellous growth of the Norman power and race in Europe. The conquest of England (1066) was contemporary with the founding of the Apulian and Calabrian principalities by

AN ENGLISH KING. 61

the famous half-brothers, William Bras de Fer, and Robert Guiscard (1056). These conquests paved the way for the greater enterprise of Godfrey de Bouillon and Peter the Hermit within a few years after. A century later the

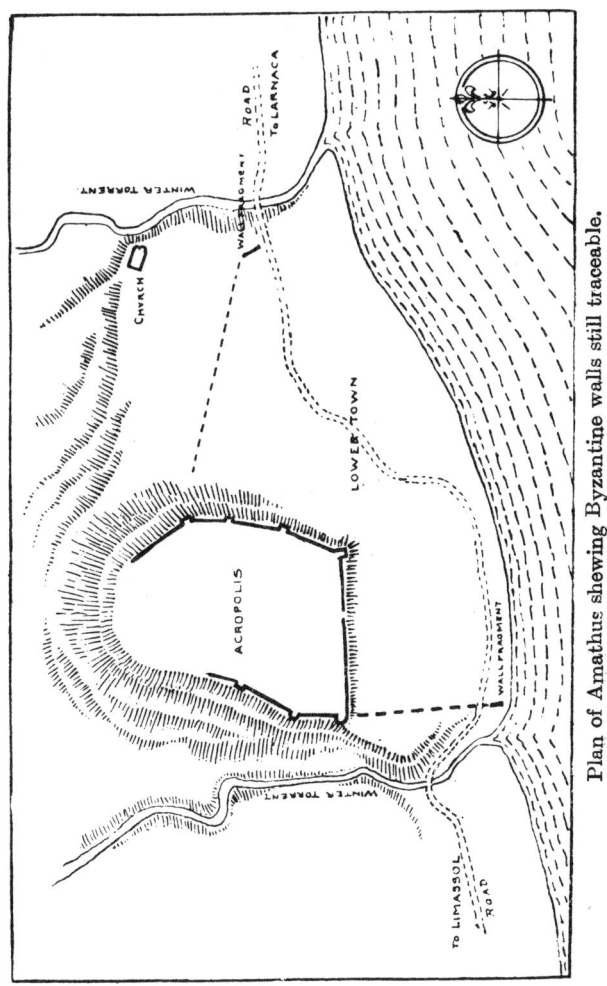

Plan of Amathus shewing Byzantine walls still traceable.

Norman Kings of Sicily had formed a magnificent feudal state out of the ruins of Magna Græcia, and its chaotic elements of Greek republics, Lombard duchies, and Saracen colonies, such as Naples, Amalfi, Benevento, Messina,

Palermo, and an innumerable series of similar communities. By the time of the Third Crusade the Norman occupation of southern Italy was firmly established, and the ever increasing race was sending forth fresh colonies for which fresh settlements became necessary. The subsequent expansion of European colonization, and the modern Europeanized world originated in Norman enterprise and energy.

The Byzantines of the eleventh century realized with fear and amazement the consequences of the great Crusades. After the first helpless efforts of the Emperor Alexis I. to divert these hordes of barbarians, as he somewhat reasonably considered them, from making use of his dominions as a pathway to the Holy Land, he and his immediate successors seemed to have succumbed to utter hopelessness, as they saw province after province become European feudal principalities. The eventual fate of Constantinople, and the last relics of the Eastern Empire in 1204, seemed foreshadowed by the narrowing limits of those dominions once ruled by a Basil, a Leo, or a Constantine of a more glorious age.

Isaac Comnenus, as the despot of Cyprus, indulged all the cruelty and the vices which his position and natural inclinations encouraged. Niketas Choniates has left a vivid picture of the tyrant. He was the most irritable of men, and in his fits of excitement emitted strange bubbling noises, whilst his lower jaw trembled with agitation. He exceeded the Emperor Andronicus as much in the cruelty of his character, as Andronicus surpassed the most notorious tyrants who ever existed. He was hourly stained with the murder of innocent persons, and this shameless and abandoned wretch passed his time, moreover, in adultery and the debauchery of young girls.

Neophytos the hermit of Enclystra states that for seven years the island groaned beneath this scourge of fate, that he reduced the Cypriots to such a state of despair that all were ready to welcome anything which afforded a means of escape from such a tyranny. At the same time the venerable Orthodox hermit regarded the coming of the Latins as a not unmixed blessing; to him they appear as the "wolves" to be classed as little better than the Saracen "dogs."

AN ENGLISH KING. 63

Both the despot and his unfortunate subjects were equally alarmed on hearing of the arrival of the Anglo-Normans on the coast of Cyprus. But for the unexpected accident of the shipwrecked crews having been illtreated—a customary thing in those days—no reason for hostility by the Crusaders would have existed, nor an excuse for an attack on their part which there was now every reason to dread. In spite of what he must have evidently foreseen, the despot maintained a bold front until the last extremity when his fate was sealed by an ignominious capture and surrender.

The fears of Isaac Comnenus were justified by the records and the memories of Cypriots then living, who had both witnessed and suffered the atrocities committed by Raynauld de Chatillon, Prince of Antioch, in the middle of the twelfth century. At that earlier date the Greek emperor had been sufficiently strong successfully to enforce a compensation for the raid, but in 1191, the ties of dependence between the despot of Cyprus and the Greek Empire being severed, no help could be expected from Constantinople.

For twelve days the small English squadron under the command of Stephen de Turnham, rode at anchor before the town of Amathus, without news of the fate of the rest of the fleet. Before the eyes of the Anglo-Normans rose the once famous acropolis on which a temple of Venus Amathunta had in ancient times attracted the pagan devotee or the Phœnician trader to the shore, but now was crowned with Byzantine towers and walls of rough masonry, above which floated the blue and white banners of the Eastern Empire. The plan of the Byzantine city of Amathus might be fancifully compared to the form of a capital A, in which the upper triangular space represented the acropolis citadel pointing inland, whilst the two legs or extremities of the figure were formed by two flanking walls connecting the triangular upper town with the seashore, and enclosing a large space of sandy beach on which the smaller craft and galleys could be drawn up when stormy weather threatened. The place had a forbidding air, and although the lower part of the city seemed somewhat unprotected from seaward, the long line of wall with its many towers, forming the south or visible side of the acropolis, was of a sufficiently imposing character in the twelfth century.[1]

On May 6th 1191, being the festival of St. John *ad portam Latinam* and a Sunday, whilst the two queens and their attendants were still hesitating about paying a visit to the Despot on shore—they had already given him an ambiguous promise to do so on the morrow, and the whole party of English and Normans was agitated by intense anxiety both as to the intentions of the Greeks, and the possible fate of King Richard and the main fleet—their suspense and troubles were suddenly put an end to in the happiest manner. The watchers seaward about midday espied two ships upon the horizon bearing down upon the scala of Amathus. Soon they displayed the Anglo-Norman ensigns to the joy of the little company of the English in the bay, and as they drew nearer, the horizon behind them could be seen filled with the whole of the main fleet, sailing with rapid course and in good trim for the same destination. The joy of the reunited warriors and their attendants was naturally exuberant, and the clang of trumpets and the beating of drums was sufficient to strike terror into many a Greek amongst the crowds on shore.

---

[1] Phœnician Amathus was a famous city in its time, and even so late in history as the days of the Romans, gave the name of Amathusia to a great part of Cyprus. The Phœnicians—greatest traders and slave dealers of prehistoric times—seem to have been like other Semites, singularly deficient in any artistic sense, and have hardly left a monumental trace of their presence in any of the innumerable ports of the Mediterranean where once their commerce flourished. Amathus is supposed to have been the first Phœnician colony in the island, (Cesnola " Cyprus," p. 21), but in spite of its importance and distinction, its Phœnician remains would be difficult to define.

Hellenic culture seems to have penetrated the Phœnician world at an early period, much as the Roman civilization was adopted by the Semites at a later time. To Hellenic influence must be attributed the colossal stone vase—the famous " Vase de Amathonte," now in the Louvre—which was at one time the great attraction for the archæological visitor to Amathus. In 1866, this vase was removed to Paris by a certain Lieut. Magen, a naval officer with an ambition to distinguish himself as an archæologist. This remarkable vase was presumably one of two standing at the entrance of a Phœnician temple for lustration purposes, and recalls the use of such vases in the Jewish temples of different periods. To how many uses may it not have been applied in the course of the milleniums which have passed since it was first dedicated to the rites of Astarte or Ashtaroth. Standing perhaps as the " Phiale " in the courtyard of a Byzantine church when the English entered the city in 1191, King Richard may have dipped his fingers in its holy water, oblivious of anything beyond its Christian use.

In Phœnician Amathus the cult of Venus was apparently somewhat unique : according to Cesnola (" Cyprus," p. 132), it was represented by a female figure with a beard !

AN ENGLISH KING. 65

King Richard was received with acclamations, and after visiting the royal ladies on board their dromon he proceeded to hold a council of war in his own galley. At this council the news of the barbarous manner in which the three shipwrecked crews had been treated, and the general hostility of the natives of the island, was considered a sufficient cause for demanding satisfaction and compensation from the Despot, without delay.

On the following day, being Tuesday, May 7th, two knights were accordingly sent with an amicable message to the Despot demanding compensation for the injuries received, and the return of the money and goods which had been plundered by his subjects. On hearing this message from the ambassadors the despot broke out into very abusive language, speaking in a disdainful manner of the English king, and boasting of his own imperial character, and declaring that he was alone responsible for his actions, he refused to comply with any such demands. "Pruht, sires, who is this man you call your king?" he is said to have exclaimed.

The two knights returned to King Richard with an account of the Despot's reception of their message and of his arrogant behaviour, whereat the king was justly irritated, and immediately shouted "To arms," a command which his men were only too willing to obey. Preparations were immediately made to land the troops and attack the town of Amathus, and for this purpose the small boats attached to the galleys and larger vessels were supplemented by fishing boats attracted to the spot by the prospect of being employed for such an object.

The attack by the Anglo-Normans had been prepared for by the Greeks during the preceding fortnight. The long stretch of sandy shore between the two extremities of the side walls which bounded the town towards east and west, and constituted the "scala" or landing place as above described, had been barricaded with timber palisading together with some old boats drawn up on shore, and with all kinds of bars and obstacles best adapted to prevent a landing taking place.

Behind this barricade, as a first line of defence, were stationed archers and slingers ready to shoot at their assailants as they came on shore; as an additional impediment to the landing they had a few galleys close to the barricade filled with young men experienced in naval fights and well armed.

As the Anglo-Normans began to approach the shore in their small boats they suffered very much from the arrows of the enemy, and they quickly discovered their only chance of success was in rapidly coming to close quarters. Their first effort was to drive off the slingers and archers in the galleys along the shore. This they did without much trouble, the Greeks jumping overboard and trying to hide from the Norman crossbows underneath their vessels. The Crusaders at last effected a landing and began to drive the defenders from the barricade, but the whole city seemed to swarm with men, and the defence by means of engines throwing stones and darts, and the immense number of archers almost seemed to render the event doubtful.

King Richard, ever foremost in any fight, was naturally to be found amongst his men in the boats. When he observed the slow progress that was made in driving the enemy from the barricade, and the pertinacity with which they maintained possession of the shore, he ordered his rowboat to be beached and as the keel took the ground he leaped into the shallow water with a few of his followers, and instantly began hewing down the Greeks who had the temerity to attack him. His example was quickly followed by the rest of the Crusaders, and the execution done amongst the enemy soon cleared the barricade of all its defenders. Meanwhile the archers who remained on board the galleys and small boats sent repeated flights of arrows against the retreating Greeks who still offered some resistance at the wall dividing the upper town from the beach or "scala."

Once the Crusaders had obtained a certain foothold on the land they soon proved themselves invincible to the unfortunate natives. Their warlike habits and training, the superiority and weight of their arms, great swords, and battle-axes, in a very short time caused a general panic amongst their enemies, and after being driven into the upper town, the Greeks fled in confusion into the open country. The city of Amathus had thus been taken within a few hours, and the rest of Cyprus then lay open to the first regular occupation by Europeans.

AN ENGLISH KING.

The upper town or acropolis was now deserted by its defenders and the Despot and his army were in full retreat, but the Anglo-Normans had no cavalry with which to pursue them. Although there were plenty of horses on board the fleet, owing to the impetuosity of the king and the difficulty in landing them, the only horse which could be found even for the king to ride upon was one furnished with a pack-saddle and rope stirrups, on which Richard vaulted with the idea of carrying on some sort of pursuit, but this was of course impossible under the circumstances. The town of Amathus thus rapidly occupied by the Europeans, became as was usual in those days after a siege, a scene of rapine and pillage amongst the native houses, but there were also many representatives of foreign interests in the island, whose persons and properties had to be duly respected.

The occupants of the European houses were careful to keep within their walls and securely barred gates, until the turmoil and disturbance in the streets and lanes of the native quarters should cease.

The attack on the seaport of Amathus had been sudden and decisive, the rout of the hostile native army was complete, and nothing remained for the Anglo-Normans to do beyond settle down for a while to refresh themselves after the excitement of storm and warfare through which they had recently passed, and before proceeding with the complete subjugation of the island.

The complete occupation of Cyprus was now regarded as a *fait accompli* by the Crusaders. The possession of the island was expected to prove a most valuable support in future campaigns for the benefit and the interest of the crusading kingdom of Jerusalem, and so, as a matter of fact, it did become the visible and positive representative of a somewhat visionary kingdom of that name for the next three centuries. But for this occupation of Amathus by the Anglo-Normans in 1191, the titular kings of Jerusalem would have been obliged to seek an asylum in Europe, and the Latin interests in the Levant would have been proportionately diminished by an abandonment of the crusading ideal.

The above description of the landing at Amathus follows our author Vinsauf. Mas Latrie, on the authority of the "Continuator of Will. of Tyre," states that the

Anglo-Normans disembarked on the sandy beach near by, and then advanced on Amathus by land, and were astonished to meet some resident European merchants who informed them that Isaac Comnenus had abandoned the place in a panic. But the spirited account by Geoffrey de Vinsauf seems more in harmony with the rest of the story, and is moreover supported by Richard of Devizes.

The Latin Kingdom of Jerusalem was as much opposed in a general way by the native Christians as by the Moslems, and the more or less hostile attitude of the Greek emperors towards the various bands of pilgrims which had passed through their dominions ever since the beginning of the Crusades, had brought about as great an enmity between the eastern and western churches as any which existed between the respective followers of the Cross and Crescent.

Meanwhile the Despot of Cyprus, Isaac Comnenus, was still at liberty, and capable of retarding the settlement of this new Latin colony and possession. He was known to have a secret pact with Saladin, and his treachery and malevolence had within the last few days been sufficiently displayed.

The first care of the Anglo-Normans in their new quarters was to guard against any surprise attack by the Cypriots, and men-at-arms were accordingly stationed under competent knights at all the entrances of the town. The native women and children who had been abandoned by the Despot and his followers, and the few priests and aged and infirm non-combatants left behind were provided for, and the temporary arrangements of a camp of occupation were proceeded with. The principal house in Amathus, the residence of the Despot, and a place of trifling importance, but little larger than the other mud walled native houses, was prepared for occupation by the royal personages of the Crusade. Here within enclosures of sun-dried brick, were courtyards planted thick with fruit-trees, and surrounded by the dark windowless rooms and cloisters: muddy water-leets meandering through a jungle of vegetation gave a squalid, deplorable appearance to the interior. The huge *alicate* or water wheel for drawing water seemed to fill up one of these enclosures. To the Normans, accustomed to the solidly built castles and homesteads of their native land, these miserable mud

AN ENGLISH KING.

hovels of a southern race were objects of contempt and derision. They viewed with disdain the prospect of having to put up with such poverty-struck quarters in a country which they had been induced to believe was both wealthy and civilized. The knights and ladies of the Crusade having landed and exchanged the cramped confinement of shipboard for the pleasanter if somewhat squalid accommodation of Amathus, the fleet of more than two hundred ships was left to ride at anchor in charge of the seamen and horseboys.

On May 8th, 1191, the spectacle presented by the roadstead of Amathus was animated and gay: the blue waters of the eastern Mediterranean were covered with the almost innumerable ships of all sizes and kinds, from dromons and busses or cats, down to the galleys and longshore fishing craft, conveying the crowd of English and Norman Crusaders and pilgrims on their enthusiastic quest to the Holy Land. Reflected in the brilliant water were the furled sails, whilst from the mastheads floated a variety of banners and streamers. The pennons of feudal lords marked the ownership of many ships, but the majority bore either the banners of the great military Orders—the black and white of the Temple, or the red and white of the Hospital—or the red cross on a white field, the recently adopted cognizance of the King of England, which has ever since been the national flag of our country.

Overlooking the busy scene from the acropolis, the Crusaders were impressed with a sight which filled them with thankfulness for the success of their journey, for their escape from the recent storms which had so much imperilled it, and for the happy augury of this easy conquest of the centre of the Levant, the very key of this now to be re-established holy Kingdom of Jerusalem. As they surveyed the ships with pride and exultation, they felt themselves to be members of an invincible armada on a path of conquest in which Cyprus was to be a principal stronghold, and in future a secure and convenient port of call.

With the deeply religious bias of the period they set at once about offering solemn Te Deums to the Divine Power which had so manifestly favoured them, and with this object in view both the Orthodox and Latin churches of Amathus became objects of the greatest interest to a crowd of devotees.

GIBELET

CHAPTER VII.

AMONGST the foreign residents in Amathus at this period were many Italians, citizens of the great republics of Venice, Genoa, Amalfi, Pisa, etc. These people formed most important corporations of merchants, engaged in the flourishing commerce of the Levant; like the members of the chartered Levant companies of a much later date they lived together in communities within strongly walled enclosures or *fondacci*, within each of which was a Latin church of some importance. In 1148, the Byzantine emperor Manuel had granted a special charter to the Venetians for the establishment of their *fondacco* at Amathus,[1] and the Amalfitans enjoyed similar privileges, both of these republics being in close political and commerical relationship with the Byzantine Empire. As already mentioned, these Europeans were careful to keep within their respective compounds during the attack on the town, assisting neither party, but immediately on the cessation of hostilities they naturally threw open their gates and fraternized with their brother Latins.

The Orthodox monks and priests who had remained behind in charge of their little churches, when the rest of the natives had abandoned the town, although but little disposed towards friendliness with the invaders, soon perceived that their safety and well being could only be secured in a due acknowledgment and swearing of fealty to the northern king. Already this new " sovereign

---

[1] Heyd: " Colonie Italiani in Oriente," II., p. 287.

AN ENGLISH KING. 71

lord," who had so suddenly appeared upon the scene was being hailed by some as a welcome deliverer from the barbarous tyrrany of Isaac Comnenus.

The city of Amathus in the twelfth century possessed an Orthodox cathedral of a Bishop, secondary only to the Apostolic Metropolis of St. Barnabas at Constantia, or as it was afterwards called Famagusta. Within this cathedral church was the shrine of St. John the Almoner, one of the chief saints of Cyprus, and the particular patron saint of the great knightly Order of St. John afterwards so famous in Mediterranean warfare. In the dark and impressive interior of this church, with its vaults covered with obscure paintings from which the figures of saints and angels in their distorted outlines loomed undefined and etherial in the flickering lamplight—for of daylight there was little but what found its way through the small window slits—the black robed bishop and his attendant monks had taken sanctuary. Standing in front of the great iconostasion, with his pastoral staff in one hand and a small silver cross in the other he was engaged in calming the excited crowd of women and children collected together within the shadows, on the day after the Crusaders' landing.

Outside the church in the sunshine flooding the street was a crowd of European pilgrims and men-at-arms, who from the direction of their glances and gesticulations seemed desirous of entering the church, the doors of which had been closely barred and fastened. A knight of superior rank amongst the pilgrims volunteered to pacify the fears and overcome the opposition of those within the church to the ingress of the crowd without, and an interpreter having been procured for the purpose the Europeans were at length admitted within the sacred precincts.

The bishop and his monks satisfied of their own personal safety considered it wise now to encourage the throng in its devotion to the sacred relics of St. John, and conducted the crowd to a kind of small chapel built against the southern wall of the church, within which was a large tomb of simple masonry, filling up the interior. This chamber, which admitted of a very few devotees entering at a time, was completely dark but for the three or four twinkling oil lamps suspended from its roof. The atmosphere was dense and oppressive, and would have overpowered less vigorous lungs than those of a mediæval pilgrim. Candles were distributed amongst the crowd, and their flickering glare caused strange effects of light and shadow amongst the varied forms, habiliments, and strongly marked features of the crowded faces of the devotees. Against the dimly lighted walls the shadows of men and women seemed to dance amongst the painted forms of grim saints and heavenly personages, with the towering figure of St. John himself and his attendant damsel conspicuous above the rest.

Within this chapel the northern visitors made their prostrations and knelt in all the fervour of their ardent faith, whilst the guardians of the shrine, standing aloof, seemed to insist on an even greater distinction between the two great branches of the Catholic Church than in reality existed.[1]

The crowd of Anglo-Norman pilgrims and the knights and ladies who had landed from the fleet, thronging the narrow mud-walled lanes of Amathus, afforded a strange contrast with the native Cypriots or such of them as still remained behind after the débacle of the Despot's army. Most of the men were armed and wearing their coats of mail or leather jerkins, whilst the ladies were in their travelling dresses of homespun, and wearing the long veils of white or coloured linen customary in their native land— sad coloured figures compared with the Greek women, who with their elaborate and barbaric display of gold and silver ornaments, seemed very different from their western sisters. The effect was somewhat bizarre and strange to both parties.

The customary looting of a conquered town on the preceding day had been stopped, as far as might be, by

[1] A very remarkable characteristic of mediæval Christianity was its intense veneration and love of saintly relics. For two or three hundred years this sentiment had been growing up in Christendom and in the twelfth century hardly a church of even small importance would be considered as consecrated without its loculus or reliquary. The Crusaders displayed a particular avidity for such things, and so long as the relics shown to them in foreign countries were of a distinctly Christian character the credulity with which they were regarded was unbounded. This relic worship with all its attendant priestcraft and inevitable fraud may perhaps be allowed to have had a mitigating influence on the inter-racial antagonism of the Levant, for it is a very remarkable thing to what an extent the different sects of Christians, often holding each other as apostates, or at least as heretics and schismatics, seem to respect the ownership and the supposed authenticity of each other's possessions.

AN ENGLISH KING. 73

King Richard and his immediate officers the marshals of the army; foodstuffs had been appropriated, and many a bale of fine cloths had already been carried off to the ships. Acts of violence had however been confined to pillage of goods, and rape, arson and murder had not been such conspicuous crimes as might perhaps have been expected. The citizens of Amathus were in fact ready to submit themselves to the inevitable, on such terms as could be best arranged. The head men or "moukhtars" of the different quarters of the town had performed such acts of homage as were customary, and had cut off their beards in token of submission. The Italian communities, represented by their bailiffs, or as they would be called in a later age "consuls," were naturally disposed to receive the Crusaders with those mixed sentiments which constitute politics at all times, and whilst they balanced the chances of greater security for their commercial interests in the development of an European military occupation of the Levant against the loss of their exclusive control of the trade between Europe and Asia, they were obliged to remember the fact of their community of religious faith and ideals with the westerners.

The representative of the Genoese Republic was of course foremost in his acts of allegiance to the particular friend of his government and the customer of her great banking speculation.

The bailiff of the Amalfitans was amongst the first of the Italian representatives to approach the royal court now established in the place of the quondam government of a Greek despot, and his courteous offers of assistance and support for the maintenance of order were received with due acknowledgment by the king and his lieutenants.

The merchants of Amalfi had on more than one historical occasion displayed their generosity and public spirit in connection with the pilgrimages to the Holy Land, and it was to their initiative in a previous century that the great Order of St. John of Jerusalem owed its origin. The Republic of Amalfi was to a great extent Greek or at least Byzantine in its earlier history, but it had gradually acquired a more western character, and by the middle of the twelfth century it seems to have passed entirely under the growing Norman influences of the south of Italy.

Dressed in a magnificent robe of purple silk embroidered in many colours, and with a golden chain of office beneath his venerable grey beard, this representative of eastern commerce impressed the Crusaders with the affluence and social importance of the rich Italian traders of the period. He was received with the greatest respect, and invited to express his opinions on the new situation of his community under the circumstances of the moment.

The bailiffs of the Venetians and Pisans quickly followed in the footsteps of the Amalfitan representative, and were received on a similar footing. They all expressed their satisfaction with the novel turn in events, and their willingness to profess allegiance to the new Anglo-Norman occupation.

The churches within the European compounds had been thrown open to the pilgrims, and one of the principal topics of conversation between the bailiffs and the newcomers was the making of arrangements by which the solemn processions and Te Deums might be performed with all due dignity by the conquering Crusaders, in the manner customary on the capture of an enemy's town. These matters were naturally left very much in the hands of the ecclesiastical lords whose presence in the Third Crusade must here be more particularly referred to.

Amongst the higher prelates of the Latin Church accompanying the King of England were the Archbishop of Auch, Primate of Aquitaine, the Bishops of Evreux and Bayonne, and many others. Amongst the lesser dignitaries was a canon from the Chapter of St. Paul's Cathedral, London, who was charged with a particular commission by that representative body of the English Church to institute the charitable and military Order of St. Thomas of Canterbury in Palestine. Most of these ecclesiastics were indistinguishable from the warriors they accompanied, or from the military monks of the Temple and of St. John. Their religious character did not prevent them from entering the battlefield, or from slaying with the temporal sword, whilst at the same time the spiritual weapons of anathema and interdict remained also in their hands. Each ecclesiastic was accompanied by his levy of feudal retainers and knights, as well as by numerous clerics of low degree, more qualified to act as soldiers than cloistered monks, and possibly attracted

AN ENGLISH KING. 75

by the more congenial life of camps and taverns. In other words there was nothing sacerdotal about the appearance of a cleric on such a pilgrimage; like the layfolk, his companions, he was always booted and spurred and with a chainmail hauberk on his shoulders, ready to take his part in any scrimmage which might be taking place in the course of the great adventure.

Within a few days after the eventful 6th May, 1191, and the landing of the Anglo-Normans at Amathus, order had been to a great extent restored, and the newcomers had established themselves in the abandoned native houses, glad of the welcome change from the cramped quarters on shipboard. As already mentioned the royal personages had been accommodated with the Despot's former residence, and the great lords and bishops found lodgings sufficient for their use. In charge of the royal household was the king's steward and treasurer, his beloved and much trusted Stephen de Turnham. Amongst the noble seigneurs were Robert, Earl of Leicester, with his devoted friend, Robert of Newbury; Roger de Hardecurt; the Lord of Stuteville; and many another whose name has passed away into the oblivion of the majority—into the forgotten history of those stirring times, in spite of their deeds of valour and prowess in Palestine at a later date.

Meanwhile, after the first débacle of the native army, and the flight of the Cypriots in different directions, the Despot, Isaac Comnenus, had retreated to a position at some miles distance from Amathus on the way towards Constantia and the centre of the island. This was probably a place now known as Chirokitia. Here he endeavoured to rally his demoralized forces, and prepare for another struggle with the invaders. He felt to some extent secure so long as the Anglo-Normans remained without horses with which to attack him. But this sense of security was of very short duration, as the King of England had no time to spare on his voyage, which had already lasted much longer than he had anticipated, and the demands for his presence in the Holy Land were insistent, for his counsellors were constantly referring to the King of France as his successful rival in securing the prizes of the Crusade.

In spite of the difficulties of such a landing place the horses on board the dromons or transports were landed, and in a short time had recovered the use of their legs sufficiently to allow of their being drawn up in battle array. The animals—such of them as had not been too much injured by the long sea voyage, and the rough stormy weather—displayed their enjoyment of a return to terra firma, and the knights in their shining coats of mail, their gaudy armorial blazonings, and with pennons of every hue fluttering in the breeze, made up a gallant sight as the Anglo-Norman army issued from the land gate of Amathus in the brillance of a May morning. The men-at-arms, or infantry, had been divided into two sections, one to remain in Amathus as a guard for the fleet and baggage, the other to accompany the king and his knights on a foray of the island.

The road, of about five miles, which had to be traversed in pursuit of the flying Despot, lay for its greater part on the southern shore, where the foothills of Mount Troödos form undulating ridges and shallow valleys of chalky marl thinly covered with the dark foliage of the carroubiers and the brilliant flowering bushes of oleander. Insignificant streams, which at this season were almost dry, and hardly sufficient to supply drinking water, frequently crossed the road, but there was no impediment to the rapid march of the troops through the district. As at the present day, so 700 years ago, the same arid landscape of early summer, the same stony paths through the thorn and shinia bushes, and the same purple sea closing the distance, presented themselves to the view of the Anglo-Normans, and possibly reminded them of Provence and Languedoc to which the scenery bears some slight resemblance.

The Crusaders' advance guard came suddenly upon the Greeks encamped at the bottom of a wide valley, where a stream formed a certain amount of protection against the expected attack from the west. Their approach was immediately hailed with clamourous shouts and the usual blowing of horns and beating of drums, the means so commonly employed in savage warfare all the world over for purposes of impressing an enemy. The Anglo-Normans did not however betray any trepidation at the sight of the immense numbers encamped, and still less at the warlike shouts and gesticulations of their adversaries.

AN ENGLISH KING. 77

The party of knights was in advance of the main body of the Crusaders' army and the main guard of men-at-arms with its usual accompaniment of camp followers and ragamuffins was still a mile or two behind. Several of the seigneurs seemed disposed to counsel the prudence of delaying any attack upon the Greeks until the usual support of the infantry with crossbows, pikes, and battle-axes could be brought into action. The number of the knights on horseback surrounding King Richard amounted to but fifty whilst the enemy appeared to be several thousand strong, and their archers and slingers formed a formidable adjunct to the cavaliers, although the fighting strength of the Greeks may have been small compared with the Anglo-Normans.

The king's party of knights had advanced incautiously, or had not been properly informed of the whereabouts of the enemy—in any case the only thing to do was either to stand their ground as well as might be, or to make an impetuous charge and trust to a favourable result. The latter course was adopted by the king.

The moment was one of those tense and critical ones which were common in the course of King Richard's crusade. Instant action had to be decided upon, and the singular temerity and recklessness of the king's character naturally induced him towards a display of that daring and hardihood for which he was always celebrated, rather than by falling back upon the main army to give the enemy any encouragement, or invite an attack.

As was so often the case in after experiences in Palestine, the impetuous nature of Richard served him well, and fickle fortune favoured the often rash and very impromptu bravery of the lion-hearted one, where a cleverer general would have met with disaster as a result of strategy and caution.

King Richard, completely clad in chain-mail, and holding a stout lance in his right hand, his long-sword counterbalanced by a heavy mace at his saddlebow, and a triangular shield protecting his left side, was in excellent fighting trim. Having ordered an immediate attack on the Greeks in spite of the apparent reluctance of some amongst his followers, he cast a glance around him and shouting the new battle-cry " Saint George Aie " which had first resounded with so much effect in Sicily, he dashed forward and in a few moments was upsetting the astonished Greek cavaliers on all sides of him. Trailing after him came the fifty knights well armed and equipped with their long lances which as they broke or became entangled on impact with their enemies were thrown aside, and the terrible maces and longswords were brought into action. The execution done upon the main body of the Greeks was so sudden and unexpected that already they began to waver and give way, and being driven back amongst the tents and cabins of their encampment they became confused in an unmanagable crowd without any efficient head or any order and discipline.

The rout of the Greeks was soon completed by the news that the main body of these terrible Crusaders was rapidly approaching. In spite of the frantic endeavours of Isaac Comnenus, who was stationed on a neighbouring hilltop, to encourage his troops, and to form a rally, they gave way on all sides, and were to be seen flying from all parts of the camp, whilst the steel clad Normans on their heavy war horses chased them amongst the tents like hawks amongst pigeons. A panic fear had taken possession not only of the ill-armed peasantry but also of their master, and it was not long before the Despot himself was seen to flee on his favourite horse in a very craven manner, followed by the last relics of his army.

With the arrival of the main body of the Crusaders the fighting terminated, and the deserted camp was quickly overhauled by the victors, all classes in the army, including King Richard himself, keenly intent upon securing such a rich reward for their prowess. One of the first things which the king seized as part of his share in the spoil was a richly embroidered banner standing by the side of the Despot's tent; this he caused afterwards to be packed up and sent as a present or bequest to the abbey of St. Edmondsbury in East Anglia. This curious example— perhaps the first on record—of a work of Byzantine art being sent as a trophy to England, does not seem to have attracted so much attention at the time as might be expected, its subsequent history seems lost. In all probability it was a kind of eicon or sacred picture executed in needlework in the style of the famous contemporary embroidery from the Levant found in the tomb of Gunther, Bishop of Bamberg, representing the " Glorification of a

Byzantine emperor." In Dugdale's "Monasticon," II., 104, is a reference to the standard of Isaac, King of Cyprus, which Richard gave to the church of St. Edmund in 1191. (Sir James Burrough's collections.)

The spoils of the captured camp were considerable, and the fastidious tastes of the Crusaders were fully satisfied with the stores, arms, and rich furnishings of all kinds left behind. The care of so much riches was the chief motive influencing the further movements of the army, as it was felt necessary that a return to Amathus should be made in order to secure these treasures. The return march was therefore undertaken by the knights and their retainers loaded with the results of their first successful foray in the island. With shouts and acclamations the victors were welcomed back to the muddy lanes of Amathus, whilst the Grecian flags and banners were carried in triumph through the land gate, amidst a motley crowd of natives who had remained behind after the flight of the Greeks from the town, and the resident Europeans whose sympathies were naturally expressed in favour of the new development of affairs. Bullock wagons with strange wide spreading wheels, and strings of camels, all loaded with the spoils of the camp, followed in the procession, and a few wounded men, and a still fewer prisoners with a detachment of men-at-arms formed a rearguard.[1]

The return of the successful expedition was an occasion for feasting and merriment, and as evening closed in the usual celebration of the event by a festive supper followed as a matter of course. The squalid houses of the town with their enclosed gardens and dark interiors lighted up with innumerable lamps and torches, were filled with parties of soldiers and sailors, not excluding the monks and the fair ladies accompanying the Crusade, all bent upon celebrating an important victory in a mode which has been customary ever since human nature has existed.

The revelry which ensued, natural outcome of those feelings of triumph and success after such a strenuous day of action, was tinged by the ceremonial etiquette and the elaborate customs of feudal society. The seigneurs and their dames of varying degree, sovereign princes or

[1] Vinsauf, II. 33.

mere tenants of knightly fiefs, were marshalled into dinner parties in different large houses of the town. With due regard to precedence the heralds called upon the feudatories to attend their lords at the banquet, and the principal guests were of course entertained in the large courtyard of the temporary royal lodging. Here a high table had been arranged beneath a canopy for the king, the Princess Berengaria and the Queen of Sicily sitting at a separate table on his right, whilst to his left was the Earl of Leicester, and other principal barons of the Crusade with their ladies, seated under open-air arcades illumined by torches and candles.

As if the feast were in some European baronial hall instead of such uncouth surroundings, the squires and varlets of the royal household were busy with their customary services, bringing in the viands from the kitchen to be cut up on the dressoir facing the tables, or assisting the carvers and butlers who were the younger sons of counts and barons, for whom the serving at the royal table was esteemed an honour. Over all was the starlit beauty of the summer night illumined by the mild radiance of a crescent moon.

Names of English nobles who were present at this first great banquet of the Anglo-Normans in Cyprus, have come down to us across the centuries. Theobald Walter, Baron of Ormonde and hereditary Grand Butler of the kingdom was officiating in the feudal capacity from which his descendants take their proud family name of "Butler" at the present day.[1] Sir Gilbert de Lytton of Derbyshire, whose achievements at a later date in Palestine were famous, was the ancestor of many famous Bulwers and Lyttons, Sir David de Hampton of Wales, Sir Henry de Grey of Essex, Sir Fulk d'Auley, Sir Thomas Knowles, and many another noble knight famous in those days are recorded, but the majority of such names are now alas! lost or forgotten in the lapse of seven hundred years.

The names of Neville and Norreys still survive upon some fragments of tombstones in the fifteenth century

---

[1] Burke's Peerage. The Butler family was of great distinction in the twelfth century, the Baron of Ormonde's brother Hubert was the Bishop of Salisbury who was for so long a time in the Holy Land

AN ENGLISH KING. 81

churches (now mosques) of Nicosia, and it seems but probable that representatives of these old English families would be present in the Third Crusade.

The feast proceeded with the usual solemnity of the mediæval customs in such matters. The convives were decorated with wreaths of flowers which the ladies of the Crusade had been able to gather during the long day of their lords' absence outside the walls of Amathus, and roses had been scattered over the dining tables in the way customary in baronial halls. The commencement of the repast was intimated by the blowing of horns, the " corner l'eau" as it was called, as all the guests were expected to wash their hands, and receive their napkins or towels before sitting down to the feast.

The king having entered and seated himself on his chair, the seigneurs and dames took their places at the side tables ranged round the enclosure, all fronting towards the hollow square at the lower end of which were two or three sideboards forming the dressoirs supporting the plates and dishes of silver, and where the viands were cut up after being presented for selection to the king and his guests. The presentation was a piece of ceremonial : to each of the guests in their degree, from the king downward, the great dishes from the kitchen were exhibited by a varlet, one knee on the ground, whilst the seigneur carver stood by, ready to cut up the fish, meat or fowl, when it should be returned to the dresser for the purpose ; the portion was then served to the waiting guest on a slice of bread or ·toast called the tranchée or trencher, usually baked for this particular purpose, and received by him on the silver plate which served for all courses and remained on the table in front of him during the repast. Cups of silver, or silver-gilt, were filled with wine by squires especially appointed to this service, from the great hanaps or jugs filled with the vintage of Cyprus, and handed with equal formality to the assembled seigneurs, and the golden product of Paphos, praised by King Solomon the Wise, was not without its votaries. Its strong, sweet flavour and fragrant aroma pleasing the northern palates accustomed to the cider and mead of their native lands.

The lambs roasted whole with a stuffing of rice and raisins ; the boiled meat, and the bouillon ; the stewed partridges, and the fish cooked in sauce of onions, herbs, and oil, having been disposed of—with much clatter of

The site of Amathus at the present day. In the foreground is a fragment of the port defences which Richard I. carried by assault on 7th May, 1191.

AN ENGLISH KING. 83

plates and knives and spoons, but with the singular absence as we should consider it in modern times of any forks— the table cloths were withdrawn, after the removal of the saltcellars and the large bowls into which the guests had thrown bones and pieces of food which they had rejected. On the long bare tables were now placed spiced sweetmeats, and flasks of wine which the noble company consumed amidst the fumes of incense, a custom somewhat representing the coffee and cigarettes of modern days, and for those who desired a pastime the inevitable backgammon and chequers or chess, and the various games with dice and draughts were provided.

In the course of the feast, "entremets" as they were called, had been introduced. The entremet was usually some recitation or play-acting by jongleurs or poets attached to the household of a prince, but in the present case it took the form of dancing "à la Romaica," a novel scene for the northern Crusaders. Two young Greeks had been found with a special agility in the art of Terpsichore, and their gyrations and antics had met with much applause, more especially when as a contrast to their posturings and steps they took to dancing on their hands with their legs in the air, in a manner very much practised in Cyprus, and regarded as the *nee plus ultra* of the science even to within living memory.

At an early hour as we should consider it in modern times the royal party, followed by the rest of the Crusaders, retired to their various lodgings weary with a strenuous day, and the city of Amathus slept in the charge of Anglo-Norman watchmen.

For several days after the fight with the now demoralized army of the Despot, Isaac Comnenus, and the triumphal feast in Amathus, the Crusaders rested at their leisure and began to form plans for the total subjugation of Cyprus, as well as for the more ostensible purposes of the Crusade.

An edict was issued by the king and his barons that all those people in the island who voluntarily came into Amathus and took the oath of fealty to King Richard should be treated as his friends, and those who did not must be prepared to be treated as his enemies. This edict caused an immense defection from the followers of the Despot, more especially amongst the numerous Armenians at that time established in Cyprus. The men on swearing allegiance to their new sovereign were required to shave off their beards in token of their change of masters —it being the Norman fashion to shave the beard. With the increasing goodwill of the islanders towards the invaders came about opportunities for the exploring and foraging parties to extend their rides into the interior and along the coast. They soon discovered that the Despot had retired to Nicosia which, although a place of small importance in those days, seems to have been regarded in the light of a future capital of the island. Many interesting objects were observed by the strangers in these explorations, things which filled their simple minds with wonder if not with admiration. Many strange traditions and legends still lingered in days of simple faith which have long since faded away into the vast region of all human forgetfulness never to be restored, and in the majority of cases difficult to be recovered. The Paladius of Charlemagne, the saints of the Gospel, and the more ancient if less respectable associations of Venus, Apollo and Cupid, were mingled together in a strange phantasmagoria in which such characters chameleon-like assume an aspect given them by current sentiment and events. The story of Venus and Adonis to the mediæval mind, instead of a primitive nature myth with a religious significance amongst the ancient Syrians, had become a romance, and the Goddess of Love was credited with having established herself as a feudal queen of Cyprus with due succession to the crown on the part of her son Prince Cupid. The history of Queen Venus was now filled with references to battles and tumults which, whatever their abstract meaning, were regarded as a matter of course reflecting the usual life of the period. Her army was supposed to contend with some undefined enemy—of course there could be no feudal queen without a feudal army, and the presence of a feudal army naturally occasioned the appearance of inevitable enemies. For some unknown reason the forces contending with the queen's army were supposed to be under the control of twin brothers—the Diyeni, who seem identical with the Dioscuri of Roman mythology—who pursue the queen into dark caverns or on to the mountain tops. But with all this grotesque mediæval dressing up of the ancient

AN ENGLISH KING. 85

mythology there was an absurd attempt to constitute the ancient divinities into actual personages, and attach them tangibly to the history of the island. With true mediæval sentiment for memorials the most important surviving Roman sarcophagus, its sides covered with sculptured flower garlands and bulls heads was actually identified as the "Tomb of Venus," and bore this name at Famagusta throughout the middle ages. The Diyeni are still commemorated by numerous landmark stones on the ordnance map, as " Petra tou Diyeni " but their names have otherwise faded from the modern Cypriot legends.

LVSIGNAN

CHAPTER VIII.

ON the Saturday concluding the eventful week which had seen the conquest and occupation of Amathus by the Anglo-Normans, the watchers on the lookout seaward were aware in the early dawn of three ships approaching the island from the eastern horizon. Their long lateen sails seemed like purple shadows slowly moving through the deep yellow sky, and its ruddy reflection in the sea, in the early morning light. As the gorgeous colouring of an eastern dawn grew paler, and its deep colours were absorbed into the brilliance of the rising sun, these visitors displayed at their mast heads the banners of the cross, and they were descried as Christian galleys sailing on a course direct for Amathus.

The arrival of newcomers was of the greatest interest to all the army now encamped on the island, and to none more than the active and impetuous King Richard, who no sooner heard of the event than he immediately ordered out a small scout vessel, called a "saetie," into which he stepped as soon as it was ready, and caused himself to be rowed to meet the approaching galleys.

As the king's rowboat hailed the nearest ship great was the astonishment of those on board to learn that the three galleys were carrying the King of Jerusalem, Guy de Lusignan, his elder brother Geoffrey (Gaufrid) Count of Jaffa; Humfrey (Anfrid) de Turon; Bohemoud III., Prince of Antioch, and his son Raymond, Count of Tripoli; and the

AN ENGLISH KING. 87

Armenian Leo, brother of Prince Rhupen of the Mountain. Of these, King Guy was almost in the position of a fugitive from Acre, whence he had come for the purpose of claiming the patronage and protection of the Anglo-Normans against the action of the French king and his party who sought his deposition from the throne of Jerusalem in favour of Conrad de Montferrat. The other princes and nobles had come with him to swear fealty to King Richard.[1]

A brief sketch must here be given of the life and manifold adventures of Guy de Lusignan, the last Latin king to be crowned in the Holy Sepulchre church at Jerusalem, and the first King of Jerusalem to be recognised as the feudal lord of Cyprus.

The family of the Lusignans, Counts of Poitou, is first recorded in the ninth century, in the person of Hugh I. "the Hunter"; his son Hugh II. was the builder of the family chateau of Lusignan, a place which still exists as a town in the neighbourhood of Poitiers, but the venerable chateau was demolished by the Huguenots in 1574. During the tenth and eleventh centuries, the family was represented by a succession of feudal lords, all named Hugh, and in 1152, Hugh VIII., or "Le Vieux" married Bourgogne de Rancon de Taillebourg, of this marriage came Hugh IX., Count of Poitou and La Marche, Geoffrey, Count of Jaffa, Amaury and Guy, afterwards kings of Cyprus and Jerusalem. Guy was the youngest of the brothers, but although he attained to a high dignity he was not considered by any means the cleverest.

Hugh IX. continued to reign as feudal lord and Count of Poitou and La Marche, and did not participate in crusading politics, but his three younger brothers went out to the Holy Land and rose high in the adventurous society of the Latin kingdom during its period of decline and fall. Geoffrey, the elder of the three, was given the important lordship of Jaffa and Ascalon, with its fortresses of Blanchegarde, Mirabel, and Ibelin. From this donation by King Amaury I. in about 1170 sprang the fortunes of the three brothers. Like his elder brother Hugh, Geoffrey was content to remain merely the holder of a fief, whilst Amaury and Guy aspired to much higher positions or were perhaps carried into them by a turn of fickle fortune's wheel.

[1] Benedict of Peterboro.

The succession to the crown of the feudal kingdom of Jerusalem had been of a very irregular or elective character from the beginning. The great Godfrey de Bouillon had rejected the title of king, preferring that of " Baron " or " Advocate " of the Holy Sepulchre. His brother Baldwin I. had been the first regularly crowned King of Jerusalem, and on his death in 1118, the crown was offered in vain to his younger brother Eustace who had inherited the patrimony of Lorraine and Bouillon, and had no mind to sacrifice it for a kingdom of adventurers in the Levant. So with the willing consent of Count Eustace, Baldwin, the son of the Count of Rethel (Rheims) stepped into the vacant throne of his namesake, and became the third sovereign of the new State under the title of Baldwin II. The voting of the barons which had raised him to this noble position was well justified by the character of his reign, and it was well for the stability of the nascent kingdom that the disinterested advice of Count Eustace of Bouillon was taken. The new king was the beau ideal of a feudal lord: although no longer a young man he did not regard his grey hair as an excuse for inaction, and he was ever ready, a fearless horseman, at the head of his army, to conduct an expedition or command on the field of battle. Of the typical Norman or Frank appearance, a high stature, and gracious manner, he inspired those under his control with sentiments of respect and admiration. He added to these qualities a religious devotion and a strict observance of moral principles in all his affairs which seemed to recall the character of his great predecessor Godfrey.

Under the second Baldwin the Kingdom of Jerusalem rose to its zenith : but alas ! he had no son to succeed him, and so perforce the crown must descend by marriage to yet another family. With the consent of his barons, Baldwin selected Fulk V. Count of Anjou to be the husband of the eldest of his three daughters, Milicent, whilst the second, named Alice, married Bohemond II., Prince of Antioch, and the third, Hodierna, married Raymond I. Count of Tripoli.

The Count of Anjou arrived in Palestine, and was married to Milicent in the spring of 1129, and shortly afterwards the great Baldwin surrendered the reins of government into his hands and that of his daughter, and assuming the garb of a hermit within the precincts of the Holy Sepulchre, died there in 1131.

The reign of Fulk of Anjou and Milicent was of twelve years, and is chiefly commemorated by the building of the great church of the Holy Sepulchre in the French Gothic style—that magnificent monument which was to be consecrated with so much pomp and circumstance in the presence of the King and Queen of France, Louis VII. and Eleanore the "Rose of Aquitaine," and of Fulk's two sons Baldwin III. and Amaury, his successors in the kingdom, in 1149.

Baldwin III. married a Greek princess, Theodora Comnena, but died without issue, and was succeeded by his brother Amaury I. who married first Agnes de Courtenay a member of the great family of central France from which the Earls of Devon claim descent; and secondly a Greek princess named Maria Comnena. By both these wives Amaury had children; by the first he had his successor Baldwin IV. the most unfortunate of all the kings of Jerusalem for he was a leper, who died without descendant in 1184 after a reign of ten years, and a daughter named Sybilla who was married to William de Montferrat, a relative of the French king Philip II. (Augustus), in 1176. William of Montferrat died the following year leaving a posthumous heir to the throne, who eventually became Baldwin V. By his second wife Amaury had a daughter named Isabella.

With the coming of Baldwin IV. to the throne the complete collapse of the Latin kingdom may be considered to have taken place. During his short reign and before his untimely death, the disunion and break up of the European allies who in the First Crusade had formed a comparatively harmonious solidarity in face of Greeks, Turks, and Arabs, was manifest. But in spite of his bad health and of the treachery of his friends and relations, he supported with fortitude and bravery the first onslaughts of the redoubtable Saladin.

About the year 1180 the condition of the Latin kingdom was becoming so gravely precarious as to induce almost a panic amongst the Frank settlers of Palestine. Dissentions within the State and the evidences of a vastly increasing extent of power and resources amongst the now united tribes of Moslems, filled men's minds with fear at the prospect of a regency—always a period of the most intense danger in a feudal state, more especially such a feudal state as was now constituted by the Kingdom of Jerusalem and its dependencies.

A popular expression of these fears seems to have operated on Baldwin IV. and induced him to seek another husband for his sister Sibylla, who was now a widow with a sickly infant, and in a perilous position in event of his own death. His choice fell upon the young Count of Poitou and La Marche, Guy de Lusignan, and as events proved this choice was anything but fortunate. Guy de Lusignan very soon displayed an ambition which was very contrary to the interest of his stepson the legitimate heir to the throne, and for this reason Baldwin IV. having changed his mind was actually endeavouring to dissolve his sister's marriage, when he died suddenly at the close of the year 1184. In the earlier part of this same year he had solemnly crowned his infant heir and nephew as Baldwin V. in the Holy Sepulchre. This ceremony which took place either in November, 1183, or early in 1184 is described by Ernoul, one of the continuators of William of Tyre : " The King (Baldwin IV.) bade crown the child. So they led him to the Sepulchre and crowned him. And because the child was small they put him into the arms of a knight to be carried into the Temple of the Lord, to the end that he might not appear to be of less stature than the rest. This knight was a stalwart man and tall, having the name Balian d'Ibelin, one of the barons of the land." A picturesque ceremony enough, and one which was surrounded by an atmosphere of gathering troubles, intrigues, and difficulties, fittingly significant of the time.

Baldwin IV. had imagined that Guy de Lusignan would become his proctor, and the guardian of the legitimate heir in event of his death, and would also provide additional heirs in the direct line of the princess Sybilla, should her eldest born but weakling son Baldwin die prematurely. But Guy had quickly fallen into a party intrigue of certain of the barons who represented a more warlike aggressive policy in the never dormant hostility between the Franks and their Moslem neighbours. Baldwin IV. seems to have favoured the opposite, or pacifist party represented by Raymond Count of Tripoli, his father's cousin, whom he had appointed regent for the newly

AN ENGLISH KING. 91

crowned Baldwin V., whilst the custody of the infant king's person was placed in the hands of Joscelin de Courtenay the seneschal of the kingdom and his grand uncle. Guy de Lusignan was regarded by his contemporaries as a man of grasping ambition, and of little intellectual or statesmanlike capacity. He was precisely the type of man who, animated by purely selfish motives, is sure to commit blunders and mistakes when placed in an unlucky moment at the head of a party or of a State. Taking advantage of the failing health of his brother-in-law, for the king was now sick unto death, he assumed the position of a more or less avowed rebel, and his wife seems to have abetted him in this somewhat unnatural conduct against her brother and her eldest son.

The death of Baldwin IV. in 1184 was soon followed by that of the child king Baldwin V. in September 1186. The party of Guy de Lusignan, which included the Patriarch Heraclius (a man of infamous character), the Grand Master of the Temple, and the famous Reginald de Châtillon, now decided on a coup d'état in Jerusalem. The filling of the city with their followers, the closing of the gates, and the holding of a council of barons in favour of the object in view, was followed by one of the most romantic of coronations ever recorded. Raymond Count of Tripoli, the duly appointed regent of the kingdom, who had been thrust into the position of a mere party leader in course of these events, sent a spy into Jerusalem to discover what was taking place. This man returned with a full report of the ceremony within the Holy Sepulchre church in words which have come down to us in the chronicles. Reginald de Châtillon seems to have acted as the seneschal of the coronation. He demanded of the assembled barons their allegiance to the princess Sybilla as their legitimate queen, and with one voice this allegiance was acknowledged. Two crowns were then placed upon the altar, one of which the patriarch took and with it crowned Sybilla, saying the words : " August Lady, you are but a woman and it behoves you to have some man to assist you in your undertakings, take therefore this second crown and place it on the head of him who can best help you in governing your realm." As a matter of course the newly crowned queen turned to her husband standing by her side, and as he knelt before her she placed the second crown on his head, with the words : " Noble Sire, I know not where to find one on whom I could better bestow this crown." Thus, amidst the shouts and acclamations of the assembled partizans of their party were Guy and Sybilla crowned King and Queen of Jerusalem.[1] With the crowning of Guy de Lusignan as King of Jerusalem the Latin Kingdom was split up into two hostile factions. At the head of the older families and the conservative party stood for a few years the Great Count of Tripoli, Raymond ; as the mainspring of the opposition appears Reginald of Châtillon, the unscrupulous filibuster to whom the ruin of the kingdom may be chiefly attributed.

The year 1187 was marked by the death-knell of the Latin Kingdom in Palestine. In spite of a reconciliation of the two or more warring parties in the land, any attempt of united action against the now vigorous and overwhelming forces of the Moslem, was useless and too late. The battle of Nazareth at the beginning of May was followed by the complete rout of the Christians at Hattin on July 4, 1187. The surrender of the city of Jerusalem into the hands of Saladin immediately followed, and for about a year the new king Guy was a prisoner amongst the Saracens.

In July 1188, after promising to abandon his claim to the Latin Kingdom—a promise he had little intention of performing—Guy de Lusignan was set free by Saladin. He proceeded to Antioch to meet his wife, and for a year the couple spent their time in anxious expectation of a new Crusade arriving from Europe. A small army of knights and adventurers began to collect around the representatives of the ancient royalty of Jerusalem, and in the spring of 1189 the party moved southward to Tyre. But here they met with a scanty welcome : Tyre was the seat of another aspirant to the crown of Jerusalem in Conrad de Montferrat the husband of the princess Isabella, half sister of Sybilla.

The Marquesate of Montferrat—a principality lying between the Republic of Genoa and the Duchy of Milan— was governed by a distinguished Italian family represented in the twelfth century by the Marquess William III. and his four sons, Boniface ; William, surnamed Longue-Epee ; Renier ; and Conrad. Of these sons the eldest, Boniface,

[1] Chronique d'Ernoul, XI.

AN ENGLISH KING. 93

took part in the fourth Crusade (1204) and carved out for himself a kingdom in Thessaly. The second, William Longsword, aimed at a higher title, and marrying the King of Jerusalem's daughter, Sibylla, would probably have attained his ambition in becoming the *de facto* king as the husband of the queen, but he died within a year of the marriage. Of the two younger brothers Renier, who married a daughter of the Emperor Manuel, died in Palestine within a year or two of his brother William, and Conrad figured as one of the most romantic figures, even of that age.

We first hear of Conrad de Monferrat as a very young man engaged as a partizan in the disputes between Pope Alexander III. and the Emperor. He then paid a visit to the east where he was induced to assist in protecting the Emperor Isaac Angelos against a rising of rebels under an usurper named Brannus. For this service and for his conspicuous bravery he was raised to the dignity of "Cæsar," and offered the hand of the Emperor's sister Theodora, in marriage.

A life of indolence, luxury and meaningless etiquette in the uncongenial Byzantine court had however no attraction for such a fiery and independent spirit, so quitting Constantinople secretly he suddenly appeared with a few followers in a galley on the horizon of Tyre at the exact moment when that famous city was on the point of being surrendered after a long siege to the redoubtable Saladin. This dramatic event took place in the winter of 1187-88.

The story of Conrad's deliverance of Tyre and of his subsequent marriage with the princess Isabella, daughter of King Amaury of Jerusalem and Maria Comnena, whilst her husband Henfrid de Toron was still alive and a prisoner at Damascus is a curious illustration of the very elastic and opportunist morality of the middle ages—but a sufficient excuse seems to have been recognized in the need of the citizens of Tyre to secure a powerful and experienced soldier for their leader and defender. They had no use for cowards and weaklings such as Henfrid, or even Guy de Lusignan, in the critical last days of the twelfth century.

Conrad de Monferrat had married Isabella with the very definite intention of claiming the crown of Jerusalem, to which his brother William as the husband of Sybilla would have succeeded had he lived. With this object in view he soon set about attracting a following of the Syrian barons, the majority of whom were keenly anxious to throw over the ambitious but pusillanimous Guy, under whose feeble direction the siege of the great seaport of Acre was now being planned. Guy de Lusignan seems to have been recognised as the king at first, but his position was rendered singularly insecure by the death of Sybilla and her children in the camp before Acre. Conrad de Monferrat now became a positive claimant of the throne, and was openly treated as such by his adherents.[1]

The siege of Acre (the most important commercial and military centre of the Holy Land, which had been captured by the Moslems in 1187), continued with varying success on both sides for about two years. In 1191 the city was ceded to the Christian allies, and became the new capital of the Latin Kingdom, the throne of which was now a bone of contention between the different parties amongst the allies. Guy de Lusignan who had been most legitimately crowned in Jerusalem found himself confronted by a powerful pretender relying on the avowed support of the French King. To counteract the plots and intrigues of his enemies, King Guy did that which was perhaps most politic, if somewhat craven-hearted : he fled from the camp of the Crusaders besieging Acre, to meet Richard Cœur de Lion in Cyprus, whom he was evidently desirous of regarding as a protector, if not as his hereditary feudal lord under whom his family held the county of Poitou, and La Marche.

At this point the succession of events in the Anglo-Norman occupation of Cyprus must be resumed.

The three galleys conveying Guy de Lusignan and some of his friends, arrived in the roads of Amathus Bay, and the King of Jerusalem was welcomed to Cyprus with all due ceremonial fitting his rank as the sovereign of a very important mediæval state. The three ships were soon riding at anchor amidst the usual flag salutations of naval etiquette.

To the eyes of Guy de Lusignan, as he stepped on shore in Cyprus for the first time in his life, the scene must have been inspiring. Greeted by an admiring crowd of his fellow countrymen with enthusiastic shouts, amidst the

[1] Hackett, Church of Cyprus, p. 68.

AN ENGLISH KING. 95

picturesque display of bright colours and waving kerchiefs of the numerous fair ones accompanying the host, and with that all pervading atmosphere of success which was naturally so evident in the triumphant progress of the invaders of Cyprus, the change from the tedious and always doubtful struggle which had been slowly dragging its course for two years in the siege of Acre must have been truly grateful. The King of Jerusalem had but recently become a widower, Sibylla had died in the camp before Acre, a blow not only to his natural affections, for he and his queen were a couple united in a way which is rare amongst royal personages; but also to his position. The loss of his four children by Sybilla, in infancy, had prejudiced his succession to the throne by giving his enemies and opponents amongst the Crusaders, an excuse for regarding him as a mere life tenant. He was not of the type popular with the Crusaders and he had none of the advantages of hereditary rank, so that the change in his affairs must have seemed very considerable. He was perhaps induced by this time to have almost forgotten the terrible disaster of Hattin, where he had been taken prisoner amongst the dead bodies of his friends, the complete ruin of all his worldly estate and long months of incarceration in the dungeons of Damascus. His release from prison had been somewhat contemptuous, on a promise upon oath to relinquish all claim to the kingdom, but he and his promises may have been regarded as equally negligible by the powerful and magnanimous Sultan, who imagined the days of Crusades at an end now that the Franks were everywhere displaying so much that was weak and decayed in their Levantine political organization.

The crowd assembled on the beach of Amathus in acclaiming the arrival of King Guy were giving their adherence to a cause which was to become one of the most complicated matters of dynastic succession amongst the too much married heiresses of the once famous kingdom of Jerusalem. They must have accepted the theory that a duly anointed and crowned King Guy was ipso facto the legitimate owner of the title in spite of the fact that his nieces, Mary and Alice, daughters of Sibylla's sister Isabella, were next in succession to the crown according to the custom of the land. The whole matter was further complicated by the divorce of Isabella from her first husband Henfrid of Toron in 1190, who was at the time a prisoner amongst the Saracens. The Archbishop of Canterbury had protested against this divorce on his arrival in the Holy Land in 1190, and thus men's minds were divided in the matter of the rightful descent of the crown on purely theological grounds as much as on the wider issue of mere political opportunism. The divorce of Isabella was in fact repugnant to most, in spite of the casuistic excuse that her first marriage had been without her free consent, an argument admitting of little proof, and in any case sufficiently dubious in the twelfth or any other century.

Clad in a long robe of blue cloth, girt round the waist with a gold embroidered bawdric supporting a long sword, the pommel of which was decorated with precious stones, and over all a white cloak fastened on the breast by an elaborate broach or morse of gold and jewels, he wore on his head the narrow gold circlet " fleur de lisée " betokening his kingly rank. Several of his attendants, amongst whom was the standard bearer carrying the goufalon or royal banner, with its five gold crosses on a white field, wore mantles of embroidered silk, and their costume had a somewhat oriental character due to their heads being protected by wreathed " kyfyiehs " or turbans, the ends of which hung down their backs.[1]

Amongst the seigneurs attending on the arrival of the king were the great officers of the crusading army : the Constable, the Marshals, the Grand Masters of the military Orders represented by their Grand Commanders, and King Richard's famous Steward, Stephen de Turnham. These nobles conducted the king in a solemn procession from the beach into the upper town where, entering the principal or cathedral church, he knelt for some minutes in prayer in a customary manner. Then once more through the narrow lanes of the town, strewn with green leaves and decorated with bright coloured flags and tapestries, the crowd with the king at its head and preceded by the royal officials, wended its way to the lodging of Cœur de Lion, where the two kings had a long and engrossing conference. Meanwhile the suitable lodging for a king was being prepared in one of the deserted houses of the town and a magnificent banquet to celebrate his arrival had been ordered to take place the same evening.

[1] Renaud, Histoires Arabes des Croisades, p. 528.

AN ENGLISH KING.

After much discussion between the two kings, and due consultation of the trusted members of the "Haute Cour" or Privy Council as we should call it in modern days, a general plan of campaign was settled upon. The adherence of the Templars was regarded as secure, and the opposition party consisting of the King of France, his protegèe the Lord of Monferrat, and the following of the native Frank barons who had opposed the election of Guy de Lusignan in the first instance, was secretly defied, if no open breach in their alliance could be attempted. The assistance of the King of Jerusalem, and of his supporters the Templars, in the conquest of Cyprus was welcomed and arranged for.

Once more the evening shadows of the gaunt houses and narrow lanes of Amathus were dispelled by a display of lamps and glaring torches and the sounds of revelry and a great feast re-echoed through the town, as had been the case on the return of the successful raid by the Crusaders of a week ago. Two kings now sat at a festive board upon the raised platform within the garden-compound of the royal lodging. The Anglo-Norman nobles with a few added guests sat around the enclosure, and the same somewhat tedious formalities proceeded during the course of the entertainment. The elaborate ceremonial of presenting the food and cutting it up, of guarding against the possibility of poison being hidden in a pasty or within a hanap of wine had to be observed, for did not the Saracens threaten to poison all their western enemies by means of the sugar and spices which they could alone supply them with, let alone the well-known ideas about poisoning each other which were ripe enough amongst the Christian nations. So the feast proceeded with its entremets of singing and dancing until a late hour when the retirement of the two kings signified its termination.

The arrival of King Guy on the morning of the Saturday in this most eventful of weeks in Cyprus history, was but of transient interest in the minds of the majority of the crusaders, owing to the much more important ceremony which was to take place on the following Sunday. The festival of SS. Pancras, Nereus and Achilleus which in the year 1191 happened to fall on a Sunday the 12th May, had been selected as the great day of the marriage of King Richard with the princess Berengaria. The occasion was altogether exceptional and unprecedented.

The reasons which seem to have prevented the marriage taking place in Sicily during the long detention of the crusaders in that country, are obscure and have never been explained; on the other hand the inducement to celebrate the nuptials in the comparative quiet amongst his own people landed in security on such an island as Cyprus, are self evident. In this way the dangers and difficulties which the king must have had good reason to anticipate on his arrival in the camp before Acre, were avoided. Berengaria was not only to be married, but also crowned Queen of England, so that whatever evil by chance might befall the leader of the Crusade there would be some prospect of continuing the inheritance of the crown. In the sequel fate disposed otherwise, and Berengaria died without descendants, and the crown passed to the undesirable brother-in-law John.

AN ENGLISH KING.

CHAPTER IX.

The marriage of Richard and Berengaria, and the solemn crowning of the Queen of England had been arranged as an incident of the English or Anglo-Norman occupation of Cyprus, and now that this occupation had become a *fait accompli* the joyful ceremonies must follow as matters of course. The preparations for the great event had been set on foot immediately on the decisive capture of the town of Amathus, and although very hurried were not to be shorn of the usual display and such magnificence as was befitting the occasion. A royal marriage in those days was always a matter of the very greatest political importance, and an occasion on which the largest number of feudal retainers, and especially the political partizans of the royal couple were expected to assemble. It was an opportunity for lavish display, entertainment, and largesse : sergeants and marshals were appointed to provide free quarters for the wedding guests of all degrees, and such accommodation had often to be supplemented by extensive encampments in the vicinity of the town or city where the ceremony was to take place. In the present case the Crusaders constituted a sufficiently numerous party to give importance to the ceremony, and a vast number of native notables disaffected towards their former governor, together with the foreigners established in the island added to the number.

A princely marriage in the middle ages, when quarrelsome elements in a population were sometimes displayed was often the scene of most unseemly brawls and bloody encounters, as was the famous case of the marriage of King Pepin when the invited guests finished off their feast with a regular battle, in which the King and Queen barely escaped with their lives. But such a scene was fortunately unlikely to occur in the peculiar circumstances of Cyprus, whatever may have been justly feared if the marriage had been postponed until the arrival of the Crusaders at Acre.

The bright May morning of the twelfth of the month—most auspicious of all seasons for matrimony—with its golden dawn and "old ocean's myriad smile" sparkling on the wavelets of a sapphire sea, was heralded by the blare of trumpets on the shores of Amathus Bay and the innumerable sounds of festive preparation amongst the motley crowd beginning to assemble in the lower town. The crews of the ships small and great riding at anchor were busy hanging out the painted cloths over their sides on which were displayed the brilliant heraldic devices of the seigneurs and knights travelling on board, and from every point of vantage fluttered the various banners and streamers: horns, cymbals, drums, contributed to a somewhat barbarous but sufficiently appropriate musical display suited to the joyful occasion. All who could be spared from the guarding of the town and fleet from any untoward surprise by the enemy lurking in the neighbourhood were expected to take part in the festivities.

The blazing Levantine sun, which even in spring-time seems to glow with fervent heat from the first moment of its appearance above the horizon, has rarely looked down upon a more gay and festive scene than was about to take place at the marriage and coronation of an English queen in the "enchanted isle" of so many romantic memories. Here in the Homeric legends had Venus, queen of love, floated ashore on the wavelets with their foamy crests, impelled by Zephyrus with his distended cheeks, whilst the goddess Primavera welcomed her to her new realm of spring-time and flowers. In the more historical but almost equally obscure history of ancient Cyprus the Cinyradœ, or priest-kings of the island had based their authority on this legend, and the massive ruins of the great temple which had been built to mark the landing place of the goddess-queen were still in evidence just round the corner of the Acrotiri headland forming one side of Amathus Bay. Here in later times the Cleopatras, or wives of the Ptolemies had been brought as Queens of Cyprus, on more than one occasion. Here, not far off on the same coast, had the great empress Helena landed and resided for some time, in the course of her famous pilgrimage. But none of these queens had a more remarkable experience, none of them became the objects of more singular interests, or of more romantic circumstances than Berengaria the wife of Richard Cœur de Lion in the brilliance of that May morning of the year 1191.

As was customary in those days the marriage was to take place at a very early hour—almost dawn—and the ceremony was performed within the temporary royal lodging or palace, where a very large tent had been erected in the central or garden compound of the large native house for this particular purpose. Here in the midst of a vast crowd of nobles, knights, and courtiers, not excluding many native notables who had given in their adherence to the new order of affairs, King Richard awaited his bride. The crowd overflowed the boundaries of the royal lodging and its courtyards, into the neighbouring lanes and houses of the town, and the picturesque costumes, the glitter of steel, the sparkle of occasional gems, harmonized with the gaiety and good humour visible on every countenance.

The arrival of the bridal procession escorting the princess was soon announced by the royal trumpeters, and by the beating of drums. In advance of the party appeared the representative ambassadors of Don Sancho VI. King of Navarre, the bride's father; these Spanish Grandees came to act somewhat in the position of *loco parentis*, and to assist at the drawing up of the marriage contract. Then came the royal chaplain, Nicholas by name,[1] attended by his acolytes and chanters, some of whom carried censers in their hands, others lighted candles. A bevy of noble dames and demoiselles formed the immediate escort of the bride and her principal companion, the dowager queen of Sicily, Iohanna the widow of William II. " best beloved of all the Norman race."

The ladies taking part in the wedding were all dressed in their most magnificent clothes and jewels : cloth of gold lined with miniver and ermine, stiff embroideries enclosing precious stones, and the still more precious tissues of

[1] Benedict of Peterboro.

fine silk, were displayed to the utmost extent considering that the resources available in the baggage of an army on the march were to some extent limited. The people of the middle ages had however a habit of carrying about with them their more valuable treasures. They even carried about jewels as the readiest and most secure way of providing themselves with cash as occasion might demand which would be unusual in modern days with our system of letters of credit and international banking.

Berengaria appeared in the customary garb of a lady of the middle ages—that fashion which seems to have changed so little in the course of many centuries. An undergarment of finest texture was surmounted by the long tunic without sleeves reaching to the ground, of a richly embroidered blue silk semé of golden fleurs-de-lis. These garments which fell in graceful folds about her allowed the display of her rounded limbs and elegant figure through the fineness of their texture : they were confined at the waist by a girdle of gold embroidery studded with various precious stones. On her head the princess wore the traditional wedding veil of finest white silk, confined to her brows by a golden circlet studded with pearls and entwined with a wreath of verbena which was still considered the appropriate form of the wedding-wreath. Beneath the silk veil appeared a superb mantle of cloth of gold with heavy orphreys of embroidery and gems. As was customary for a bride her hair was allowed to fall over her shoulders in rippling waves beneath the veil.

As the princess was brought into the royal tent, King Richard who had been seated on a faldstool, rose to meet her, and then conducting her into the middle of the crowd of nobles, clergy, and ladies there assembled, the marriage ceremony was proceeded with. The nuptial contract having been witnessed by the officers of State, the customary donations made, the ritual kiss given, and the two rings exchanged, whilst Nicholas the royal chaplain repeated certain prayers and the choir chanted the due responses, the ceremonial terminated amidst the shouts and acclamations of the assistants.

The sacrament of marriage being now concluded, Berengaria was obliged to face a ceremony of far more fatiguing and lengthy character—her coronation as Queen of England—which was to immediately follow on her marriage. For this purpose the assembled Archbishop and Bishops were to officiate, and the scene of the impressive ceremony was changed to the precincts of the small Orthodox cathedral which had been appropriated for the purpose.

The Bishop of Evreux, although not one of the greater dignitaries of the Latin Church had been appointed to occupy the position of chief officiant, and to place the crown on the queen's head. The Archbishop of Canterbury and the Bishop of Salisbury, who had preceded the third Crusade, would doubtless have occupied this position if the coronation had taken place at Acre, but the aged Baldwin of Canterbury had recently died there in the Crusaders' camp, and this may have been an additional reason for the holding of the coronation in Cyprus. In any case the Bishop of Evreux would be regarded as a representative of the Norman Church, and could well act as the representative of the Archbishop of Canterbury whilst the Archbishop of Auch belonged to the Kingdom of Navarre of that period. Mas Latrie states that the coronation was performed by the Archbishop of York, but this is an error: the Archbishop of York of the period was an exile (see Richard of Devizes, section 44).

The concourse assembled within the enclosure of the royal lodging and in the contiguous lanes of the town, and around the precincts of the cathedral, continued to manifest its gaiety and joyousness in the manner usual with crowds in such circumstances. The buzz of animated talk and laughter, jokes and horseplay was hardly controlled by the interest attaching to the great function on hand. Every now and then the notes of horns and drums or the softer sounds of lutes and mandolins emphasized the festive character of the hour.

The squalid appearances of a mud-built Levantine town of the twelfth century were covered over to some extent by silken hangings, eastern carpets, and the gay heraldic banners brought with them by the Crusaders; but the poor and sordid background of the scene afforded much to contrast with the substantial splendours of an Anglo-Norman city of those days. However, the brilliance of a Levantine sun compensated for much that was mean and deplorable in local surroundings.

King Richard and his bride now appeared at the gate of the royal lodging, prepared to enter upon the coronation. Berengaria continued to wear her wedding dress; the King was in his royal robes, a fleur-de-lisé crown of gold on his head, a sceptre surmounted by a fleur-de-lis in his hand. Over a vest of rose coloured stuff sewn thick with silver spangle suns and crescents which glittered in the light in a particularly brilliant manner, he wore a gorgeously embroidered robe covered with heraldic lions rampart, and fastened on the right shoulder by an elaborate broach of goldsmiths work. This robe had orphreys of embroidery enclosing many splendid precious stones, and his vest was also confined by an elaborate belt of gold plaques encrusted with jewels. Richard was in the prime of life and his muscular athletic frame and proud bearing was appropriately enhanced by the gorgeousness of his attire. With close cropped hair but flowing beard his face was lit up with a vivacious expression and a pair of piercing and unflinching eyes : on this occasion he appeared the beau ideal of the mediæval prince, the born leader of his people. His newly wedded wife was a fitting consort. Of the darker southern blood her features were aquiline and in harmony with a delicate but strong physique. Dark hair and liquid eyes with the gracious if haughty smile of the woman nurtured in a royal court and accustomed to an atmosphere of flattering ceremonial and adulation, conferred a certain grace to that beauty of youth which all women seem to possess for some period in the course of their lives.

The royal couple stood forth as types of their age : born to occupy a position for which they were well qualified, happy in the circumstances as far as might be—of their marriage, and for the moment free from the series of troubles which afterwards accumulated about the last years of the short-lived Cœur de Lion. With the conquest of Cyprus, his marriage, and his subsequent adventures in Palestine, King Richard must have enjoyed his life with a singular fulness : whether Berengaria had a similar pleasure in her rôle of a Crusader's wife has never been recorded.

The procession from the royal lodging to the cathedral was now being formed under the superintendence of heralds and marshals, and a body of sergeants was clearing the path and endeavouring to maintain some sort of order. The Bishop of Evreux, attended by the Archbishop of Auch

AN ENGLISH KING. 105

and the Bishop of Bayonne stood in front of the church portals ready to receive the king and his bride. Guy, the King of Jerusalem, with his followers, was given a place suited to his high rank.

In the procession the royal couple were preceded by a group of musicians and a standard-bearer carrying the newly adopted red cross banner of St. George. A few of the most distinguished knights and nobles with the Earls of Leicester and Ormonde came next and after them walked the king and princess, followed by a crowd of knights and ladies, far too numerous to be accommodated within the church.

On the outside of the cathedral at its west end facing the small open space and street had been erected a kind of gallery or scaffold with a small staircase leading up to it, this was to be used in an important part of the ceremony.

With the entrance of the king and princess within the dark shadows of the sacred edifice, dimly illumined by the light of wax candles in an atmosphere misty with incense, the bishops and attendant clergy took up their positions within the sacrarium behind the great iconostasion or roodscreen, with the altar in their midst. Two faldstools were arranged in front of the sacred doors of the sanctuary, and to these the royal pair were conducted, and in them they took their seats after first of all prostrating themselves at full length on the floor towards the altar.

High Mass was now celebrated pontifically with all the solemnity which such an occasion demanded and the crowded condition of the small church permitted. The opening antiphon of the " Missa pro Regibus " was chanted by the Bishop of Evreux seated on his episcopal throne whilst the cantors in their gorgeous copes, and holding their staves of office led the responses of the choir, and the Gregorian tones rolled through the vaulted interior where only the comparatively uncultivated music of the Greeks had hitherto been heard.

The gradual " Salvum fac Reginam " was shortly followed by the anointment or unction of the princess by the Bishop, for which purpose her bridal veil and wreath had to be removed by two acolytes. The Bishop then proceeded to draw with his forefinger dipped in Holy Oil, a cross on her forehead, and another on her breast, for which latter purpose the front of her dress had been made with an opening confined with a broach. The oil was then carefully removed with a linen cloth for the purpose of being ceremonially burnt by one of the attendant deacons, and her dress was refastened with the broach.

The faldstool of Berengaria was now surrounded by the Archbishop and Bishops about to confer the insignia of royalty. First of all, after certain prayers, one of the two sceptres lying on the altar was brought and placed in her right hand : with the words pronounced by the Bishop of Evreux, " Take this symbol of the Royal Authority." Then followed fifteen prayers, and at their conclusion the second sceptre, a rod surmounted with a small cross, was placed in her left hand as the symbol of justice.

The crowning was now to take place : the royal crown of gold, fleur-de-lisé and studded with precious stones which had been lying on the altar, was brought to the Bishop of Evreux, who taking it in his hands, turned to the Archbishop and the Bishop of Bayonne, the three prelates conjointly then held the glittering emblem above Berengaria's head whilst a prayer was said " Benedic Domine fortitudinem, etc." Then the crown was placed on her head, amidst the acclamations of the people within the church, echoed by still more vigorous shouts by the crowds outside.

Berengaria was now Queen of England, Duchess of Normandy and Aquitaine, and the lady of innumerable other titles which conferred on her a position in the world second to none, except perhaps the wife of the Emperor of the Holy Roman Empire, but there the Salic law created a difference.

The Queen of England had been crowned, but the ritual had not yet been completed. The " Recognition by the people " had still to be performed, and for this purpose the new queen had to be escorted by the functionaries of the coronation both ecclesiastical and civil, out of the church and on to the gallery or scaffolding which, as already mentioned, had been erected against the outside of the building. Here the group of Bishops and state officials, Constable, Seneschal, Marshal, etc., with the queen in their midst ascended by the staircase, and Berengaria wearing the jewelled crown and carrying the two sceptres was seated on a throne in such a way that all the

AN ENGLISH KING. 107

people might conveniently see her. The Seneschal then stepped forward, whilst the trumpeters sounded to command attention, and in a loud voice demanded of the crowd assembled below their acquiescence in the coronation of their new queen. Upon this a mighty shout was repeated three times, led by the choir of priests and the attendant officials : " Vivat Reginam." At the conclusion of this popular demonstration the royal party descending from the scaffold and re-entering the church, the Mass was proceeded with and at its conclusion the Bishop of Evreux addressed to the queen the three royal precepts : to preserve the peace of the Church, to restrain popular discontents, to maintain the administration of justice with mercy.

The ceremony was at length ended, the King and Queen of England returned in solemn state, surrounded by their courtiers, to the house where for the time being they were provided with a temporary home, amidst strangely foreign surroundings. The enthusiasm of the populace as the royal procession retraced its steps was unbounded, and the sounds of discordant musical instruments were mingled with the sombre tones of the simestra or gongs of the Orthodox Churches, and the bells in those of the Latin rite.

Preparations for a great feast had of course been made in such a way as to provide for the entertainment of the whole body of the Crusaders, and for a great many invited guests as well. A large number of ovens and kitchens had been constructed in the town, and all who could be pressed into the service as cooks were busy with the supplies of food which had been brought into Amathus from all parts of the island. Goatskins filled with wine were being unloaded off donkey-back, sheep and lambs were being slaughtered, bread was being baked, and huge quantities of wild turnips, (calocass) and other more or less wild roots such as seem to have constituted a great part of the mediæval cuisine were being collected into heaps. Everywhere reigned a sense of festivity and security, but at the same time there was no relaxation of watchfulness against any surprise on the part of the Griffon enemy still lurking in the north-east of the island. From the height of the Acropolis of Amathus, and its watchtowers the country inland could be surveyed for many miles, and between the town and the vineclad slopes of Troodos stretched a comparatively barren plain easy to keep under observation.

A royal feast which was to celebrate both a marriage and a coronation would represent the very *ne plus ultra* of such entertainments in any period of the world's history. It was therefore with additional pomp and circumstance that the tables were placed within the royal enclosure; the dais was now arranged for the king and queen to sit upon together, whilst a separate dais was provided for King Guy, and another for the dowager Queen of Sicily. Over these seats of importance, canopies supported on poles were erected and a hanging of rich tapestry was suspended behind them. The tables at which the gay company was about to feast were long and narrow, and bore but little resemblance to the dining tables of modern times—they were merely for eating upon, whilst the various viands reposed upon the buffets and side tables within the enclosure which served for a dining hall: the guests sat only on one side of these tables and the squire-carvers and servers presented the food across them.

The Kings of England and Jerusalem and the two Queens having retired for a short space to divest themselves of their heavy crowns and state robes, the notes of the "cor d'eau" were sounded and the marriage guests began to troop into the different places where the feast was to take place. The napkins were being distributed, the guests were being marshalled to their places behind the tables, but the busy confusion of a great feast was interrupted by the entry of the royal personages who were escorted to their places with much ceremonious attention by the officers of state. The Kings and Queens having taken their places, the rest of the company priviliged to dine within the same enclosure, the Archbishop, Bishops, and other ecclesiastical dignitaries, the officers of state, the representatives of the King of Navarre, the Commanders of the Temple and St. John's Orders, the Bailiffs of the Italian Republics, Venice, Genoa, Pisa, and Amalfi, the Genoese Admiral Grimaldi, and all the English barons with their dames, seated themselves in accordance with the instructions of the masters of ceremonies and heralds.

As on the occasion of the grand supper after the first successful raid in the island described on a previous page, the same elaborate formalities had to be gone through whilst the squires carved off the slices of meat or joints of a capon or partridge for their seigneurs and their ladies, and other squires filled their cups from great wine-jugs or hanaps. At the table of the King and Queen of England the Earl of Ormonde, as Grand Butler of the Kingdom was officiating, whilst the varlets and servers were busy presenting the dishes to their seigneurs on bended knee.[1]

With the usual sounds of joyful festivity was mingled the somewhat discordant music of trumpets, bagpipes, harps, flutes, and kettledrums or more properly speaking tom-toms, cymbals, and nacaires or the Saracen horns; an overpowering variety and number of instruments more than equal to any modern orchestra, but as they were played without much intention of forming a concert, the result was merely a great deal of noise and very little melody. Some interludes during the repast were played on lutes and mandolins accompanying the singers of a superior type of performance.

[1] Viollet de Duc.

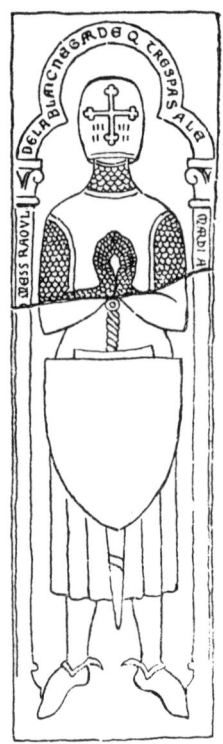

Tomb of Raoul de Blanchegarde in the Cathedral of Nicosia. Early thirteenth century [the lower part restored].

CHAPTER X.

ON the morrow of the day on which such great events had taken place a council of war was held by King Richard, the result of which was a dispatch of several foraging or investigating parties into different parts of the country with a view to locate the position of such hostile forces as were likely to be encountered in the process of dispossessing the Despot, Isaac Comnenus, of his sovereignty—a sovereignty which was in origin but an usurpation. The occupation of Cyprus had now been definitely decided upon

AN ENGLISH KING. 111

by the English king and his counsellors. The great Order of the Temple was strongly in favour of the policy—anticipating perhaps to some extent that idea of controlling the destiny of the Levant by a possession first of Cyprus, then of Rhodes, and finally of Malta, which in later centuries was successfully carried out by its heirs and successors the knights of St. John.

The exploring parties were intended to take a course which should lead to a general rendezvous in the northeast corner of the island where it was intended the Despot and his adherents failing other arrangements should be either captured or at least driven out of his dominions. For this purpose one party was ordered to proceed to investigate if possible the rocks and forest land of Troodos, by way of an important village or town called Kilani, whilst the main army of the Anglo-Normans under King Guy of Jerusalem was to march after the flying enemy in the direction of Constantia. King Richard determined that the fleet of galleys and small craft should patrol the coast and eventually assemble at the ruined port of Constantia.

Meanwhile a conference between the Anglo-Norman invaders of Cyprus and the Byzantine Despot was proposed by the Commanders of the Temple and Hospital Orders, with a view to an amicable settlement of the island as a portion of the Latin Kingdom of Jerusalem. For this purpose the Despot was induced to meet King Richard at a point on the road between Amathus and Kitium, near the former place. At this conference, after many proposals on both sides, the Despot offered to swear fealty to the King in all things, and also send five hundred men to the crusading army in Palestine, to be at the disposal and command of King Richard. He also offered to pay 3,500 marks as compensation for the robbery and violence to which the shipwrecked crews of the King's ships had been exposed before the occupation of Amathus, and to place all his castles and strong places in the hands of the King as a pledge for the due performance of these things. These proposals were submitted by the King to his council and meeting with approval were ratified in the customary way, by the King embracing the Despot in the manner depicted in the famous group of two Crusaders performing such a ceremony which has been inserted into the west wall of the Doge's Palace, Venice. After this "kiss of peace," King Richard returned to his lodgings in Amathus, and ordered that the great tent covered with embroidery which had been captured at the battle of the 8th May, should be returned to the Despot as a sign of peace and friendship, together with certain vessels of gold and silver which had been plundered with it.

By the act of swearing fealty to the English king, in presence of the crusading barons and princes assembled in the island, the Despot, Isaac Comnenus, acknowledged his dependent position under the European feudal law. But it appears that no sooner had he taken this oath of homage at the conference than he changed his mind, under the influence it is said of a certain Levantine knight named Payen de Caiffa. Who this person may have been is not very clear : he was doubtless some needy adventurer who thought to profit in a desperate defiance of the Anglo-Normans by the Byzantines, although to judge by his name he was a Norman himself and a dweller at Acre. But Payen's counsel was disastrous to his friend the Despot, and equally so for himself, and we hear no more of him.

Terrified at what he had done in acknowledging the suzerainty of King Richard, and persuaded by his evil genius, Payen, that he would shortly be cast into a dungeon, the very ill-advised Despot suddenly determined on flight from the camp near Amathus, where the conference had been held. The news of his sudden departure, with the evidences of his having renounced the solemn act and treaty of settlement which had been the object of the conference, produced alarm and disquiet amongst the Crusaders. A council of war was convened immediately, and a decision was taken accusing the Despot of perjury and the violation of the laws. Under this accusation he was held to have forfeited the realm of Cyprus, and his claims being no longer recognised, he and his followers were to be treated as outlaws.

The misguided Despot had fled from his camp on the very night after the conference, abandoning all his luxurious camp-equipment, and his horses. He had directed his journey to Constantia, which was still a town of importance, continuing to some extent as the traditional capital of Cyprus, on the site of the more ancient Salamis. But the walls of Constantia were old and ruinous, the water

AN ENGLISH KING. 113

supply which had been devised for other times and uses, could easily be cut off, and the general prospects of withstanding a siege were not encouraging. The Despot, therefore, quickly changed his tactics, and took to the open country and woods, where he hoped to carry on a sort of guerilla warfare more adapted to his needs. But his plight was very soon desperate. He was detested by a great party of his former subjects, who were even disposed to welcome the change to a foreign administration ; but those circumstances which he had least calculated upon were the indomitable perseverance of these terrible northern invading warriors, and their natural efficiency. Accustomed as the Byzantines were to the eastern races of mankind, whose strength of character and power depended chiefly on their immense and inexhaustible numbers, they now came into contact with a different type of humanity, of whom it might be said that each individual was a host in himself—in other words they were making acquaintance with the Anglo-Norman " supermen " of the period for the first time.

A guerilla war carried on in the forest land on the northern side of the island could have but a short period of duration, and end but in one way. On the precipitate flight of the Despot from Amathus, King Guy of Jerusalem proceeded on his march to Constantia, by way of Kophino and Kitium (Larnaca), and on the third day after leaving Amathus arrived at his destination which had already been abandoned by the Despot and his followers.

As the Anglo-Norman Crusaders marched across the site of Kitium, they surveyed with a certain awe and ignorant astonishment its crumbling walls and heaps of ruin, where once the busy mart of the Phœnicians had formed the first entrepôt of the ancient world.

The ruins of Kitium—the Chittim of the Bible—had a certain importance at the end of the twelfth century, and the walls and ditch of the ancient Phœnician city were still sufficiently in evidence to attract the curiosity of the Crusaders. The curious mound with the ruins of an ancient temple on its summit, overlooking the harbour where a few fishing boats still took refuge, was a landmark in the curving lines of Larnaca bay. The deserted ruins of the old city were still untouched by the speculative builder seeking second-hand building stone, and the surviving inhabitants of a once populous district were now gathered together in the huts of a fishing village which continued to exist on the site of a Christian suburb of the ancient pagan city. In the midst of this Christian or Byzantine village was a small church containing the traditional " Tomb of Lazarus." How this curious Christian tradition of the final burial place of the " twice buried " came into existence, remains an unsolved problem. Perhaps the Norman Crusaders were instrumental in establishing an Orthodox tradition which asserts that in 890 the body of Lazarus was "invented" or discovered in Cyprus, and thence carried off to Constantinople, which accounts for the present empty tomb at Larnaca.

The knowledge that so important a relic of ancient Christianity as the last resting place of Lazarus lay on the line of march, filled the more enthusiastically minded Crusaders with a desire to visit so holy a place. The King of Jerusalem therefore considered it wise to order a halt amongst the ruins of Kitium, whilst those who wished could pay their devotions at the small Byzantine church, wherein was the ancient marble sarcophagus inscribed with the words " Lazarus the friend of Christ." The Orthodox monk who guarded this church had a copious story to tell of how Lazarus after his resuscitation at Bethany was seized by the malicious Jews and sent to sea in a small boat without oars or sails at Jaffa. How he was wafted over to the bay of Larnaca by angelic means, and on his landing on the shore, the people whom he converted to the true Faith, elected him their Bishop. How he lived and died eventually, for the second time, in Cyprus, and how his tomb worked miracles.

Having satisfied their credulous faith with all this marvellous history, the Anglo-Norman soldiery once more plodded on their way towards Salamis.

The dreary scenery of this region, even in early summer, was unrelieved by the presence of inhabitants, all of whom had fled at the news of the approaching army. The harvest of the Levant had already begun, but the first stacks of corn sheaves laid on the threshing floors had been abandoned by the frightened farmers, who had also driven off their flocks of sheep and goats. Silence reigned throughout the country-side, to be broken in upon by the rude tumult

AN ENGLISH KING. 115

of the advancing army, the rough voices of the men-at-arms, the shouts and cracking whips of the baggage train drivers, and the discordant sounds of trumpets, nacaires, and tom-toms.

The way to Constantia was in those days a mere mule track leading over interminable rocky plateaux intersected by shallow gullies, in the bottoms of which grew luxuriant oleander and thorn bushes, though not a drop of water was anywhere to be found. With the exception of a few palms standing in conspicuous solitude near some deserted villages of ruined mud huts, few if any trees were to be seen in the desolate landscape. In the far distance the hard blue outline of the sea showed in violent contrast with the " russet lawns and fallows grey " of the nearer landscape, and the dark colours of the tilled fields chequering the moorland. To the eastward of Larnaca the chalky soil reflected the sun's rays in a painful glare. Thus the road continued until the sand dunes of the bay of Salamis came upon the view, and the vast marshes formed by the silted up mouth of the river Pediæs spread around the site of ancient Salamis.

On the site of the ancient city stood its Byzantine descendant—Constantia, a mere ghost of its former self, shrunken to less than a tenth of its original size. Constantia had been a capital of the island under the early Constantines, after whom it was named, but in the twelfth century it seems to have been less important than Amathus. Here the autocephalic Archbishop had formerly his cathedral, remains of which may still be traced amongst the ruins of the later town.

Constantia had this great peculiarity, that although it must have continued to a great extent the traditional trade centre or emporium of the Levant after the repeated destructions of Salamis, its defences were negligible as rebuilt by the Byzantines; its water supply, forty miles long in an aqueduct, could be cut off in a moment, and it was certainly not a place which could offer the slightest resistance to a regular army. It was merely a large walled village in the midst of ruins of both classic and Christian times, of sufficient importance to withstand a raid by pirates and slave-dealers, and relied for protection on the somewhat dubious power of the Byzantine navy.

By the time of the King of Jerusalem's arrival at Constantia, a great part of the English fleet, with King

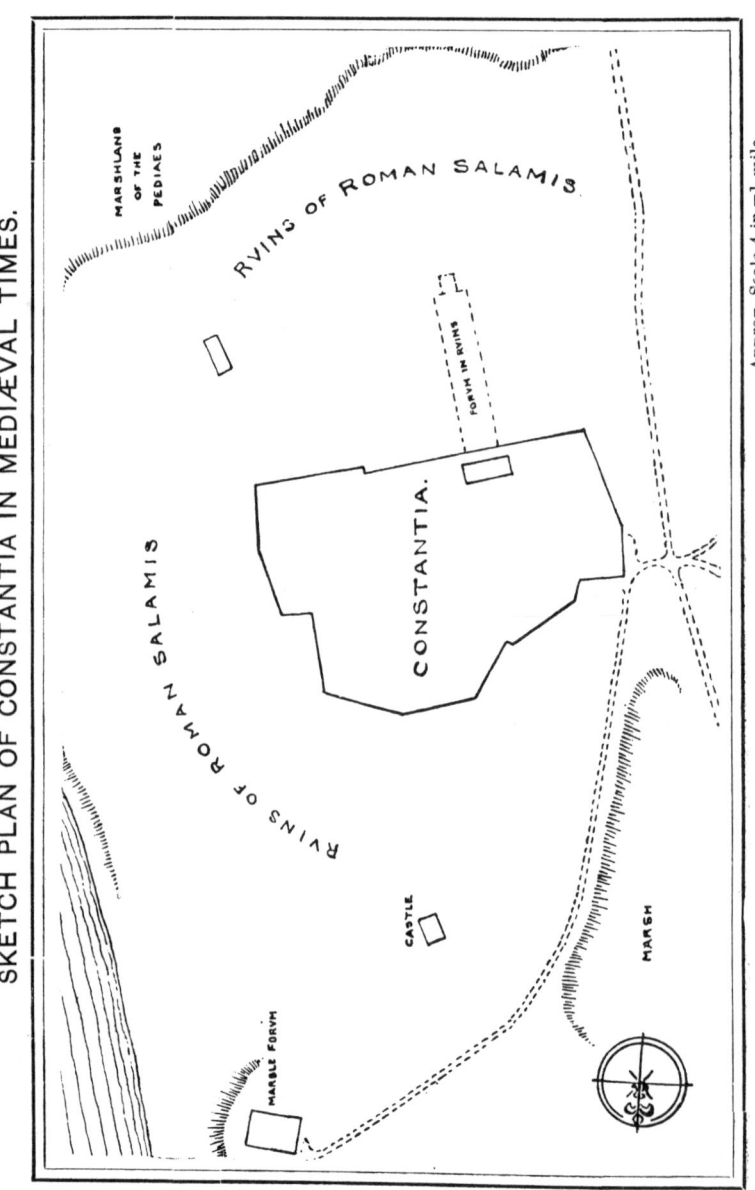

AN ENGLISH KING. 117

Richard on board, had also appeared on the scene. Constantia was therefore a centre of unusual life and activity, the sandy shore, with the ruins of the ancient port, was covered with the smaller boats and galleys drawn up, whilst the dromons and larger ships rode at anchor in the bay. The weather was propitious, summer was advancing, and the seafaring men were satisfied that the time of squalls and tempests was past. The deep blue sea of the eastern Mediterranean was sparkling under a gentle breeze, and a vast concourse of shipping, constantly increased by fresh arrivals, had more the appearance of a peaceful review than a warlike foraging expedition. Numbers of small boats attracted to Constantia as to a profitable market, had arrived laden with food supplies from the neighbouring coasts.

At their meeting in Constantia, the two kings, Richard and Guy, were immediately able to complete their schemes and plans for the conquest of Cyprus.

During these operations in the eastern part of the island, the newly crowned Queen of England remained at Amathus, surrounded by a freshly constituted court of her own, comprising the dowager queen of Sicily and many ladies who had followed their lords on the great pilgrimage.

In the early middle ages it was not unusual for a man whose taste had been awakened by classical studies, and whose powers of observation and comparison were enlarged in the course of travel, to take a very intelligent interest in antiquities and ancient buildings, and in the associations which they must always suggest.

As Master Geoffrey wandered around the market of Constantia, he now and again struck his foot against fine marble fragments of some ruined building almost entirely buried in the filthy accumulations and sand heaps. The form of a mighty column of white marble could here and there be detected, whilst the carved details of capital and cornice appeared used up in many an incongruous way on the facades of the mean buildings. In the latest rebuilding of the many which had taken place upon the site, an attempt had been made to restore some of its antique importance to the ancient forum by setting up the columns on three of its sides, but their shafts had been broken or belonged to other places, and the effect was but a barbarous patchwork.

The ruin of stately buildings thrown down by the dread earthquake, and defaced by the pitiful pilfering of their materials in a subsequent age, must always affect a refined mind with a feeling of intense regret. We moderns feel this sentiment—as we think—to its very utmost when we see the last vestiges of a vanishing and inimitable past ; but to the Benedictine wandering amongst the ruins of Salamis in the twelfth century there may have been a poignancy of sentiment even greater than to ourselves : blasé as we are with the knowledge of so many subsequent developments of taste and culture.

A Benedictine monk, quoting Virgil, Juvenal, and a host of other classic authors as the models for his own ideas, must have viewed the relics of classic art with an enthusiasm, which was perhaps either intensified or checked by the sad reflection that none of his contemporaries were able to emulate or even follow in the steps of such perfection. As he gazed around he could only feel impressed with the barbarity and the brutal ignorance of the humanity now occupying the place of a passed away civilization : all arts and crafts were once more merely primitive and savage ; all science had disappeared ; only literature survived to carry on the torch of civilization—that classic literature which admitted of those wonderful quotations which seem so odd when written in the Gothic lettering of a mediæval manuscript.

The crusading companions of Master Geoffrey were the rude uncultured descendants of the barbarians, the Goths and Gauls who had overthrown the mighty Roman Empire and all the civilization it had stood for in ancient times. To him it must have seemed a perfectly hopeless prospect— an idle dream—that such people could ever submit to the sweet influences of art in its nobler aspirations, or ever experience a feeling of reverence for a grand and magnificent past. Yet within fifty years of the moment when he was standing on the moonlit beach of Constantia contemplating the ruins of Roman Salamis, the great Renaissance spirit was being born in Italy, and like a young Hercules, gathering strength and vigour with every day and year of existence was soon to reach a maturity of even grander type than the ancients ever attained—within a few years, Abelard, Cavalcanti, Dante, would be shining amidst a myriad stars, Nicolo Pisano, Pierre de Montereau,

Robert de Coucy would be equalling the builders of the Parthenon.

As an ecclesiastic of the proselytizing Roman Church, Master Geoffrey studied the prospects of the Latin occupation of Cyprus with much interest. He observed the fanatical disunion between the Orthodox and their fellow Christians of the west, and the hopeless prospect of ever converting them from what appeared to him their insuperable errors. The schismatical attitude of the eastern Christians at this period of history was more especially irritating to a Crusader, because it destroyed that cohesion and unity of all Christendom, so necessary to withstand the enemy equally feared by all.

At the time of the Anglo-Norman conquest, the two chief capital towns of Cyprus were, as already stated, Constantia and Amathus. In addition to these a number of unfortified villages of a large size and straggling formation, built of sun dried brick, with a small church or two of more substantial materials amongst their flat roofed houses, constituted district or as we might call them " county towns." Thirteen of these larger villages were reckoned as the see towns of Bishops, or at least Chorepiscopi, under the names of Kition, Kyrenia, Paphos, Soli, Arsinoe, Lapithos, Kythrea, Tamassos, Kurion, Karpasion, Trimythos, Kerma and Nemevos. All these villages with the exception of the two last named survive at the present day, but the modern Bishops of the Cypriot Church are reduced in number to three out of the former fifteen, Kition, Paphos, and Kyrenia, whilst the Archbishop of Constantia is now styled " of Cyprus." [1]

The bishops and priests of the native Orthodox Church of Cyprus were naturally in a state of intense perturbation at the advent of these terrible western invaders. They knew, from a century of experience in the Holy Land, that where the Europeans established their feudal law and customs in the Levantine lands there was little hope for the independence and liberty of former times to survive. The Orthodox Church was in fact, perhaps the most potent influence in opposition to the spread of European culture in the Levant during the middle ages ; one has but to look

[1] This list is taken from the description of Cyprus by the Emperor Constantine (VII.) Porphyrogennetos, (A.D. 911-959) in his work "De Thematibus Orientis." quoted by Hackett in " Church of Cyprus," p. 242.

at its monuments to be impressed by this idea. In them no trace of any European influence is visible, until in comparatively modern times some belated taste for novelty or emulation has induced the imitation of misunderstood and incongrous details in a monument, producing a bizarre and even ludicrous effect.

But in spite of this evident antagonism between the two great sections of Christendom during the middle ages, and in subsequent times, certain essentials of Christianity remained the same in common between the two churches in spite of inter-racial antipathy or commercial rivalry.

On the day following the arrival of the King of England and the Anglo-Normans at Constantia, a large galley put into the bay of Salamis, flying the five-cross flag of Jerusalem. On board of it were two noble seigneurs from the camp at Acre : Drogo de Merle and the Bishop of Beauvais. At the moment of their arrival, King Richard was seated in his tent on shore, discussing the pressing business of the moment with some of his trusted councillors. On landing, the Bishop and his companion were immediately conducted to the royal presence, where, after the usual salutations on both sides, they were invited to furnish the latest news from the armies in Palestine, and to explain the object of their visit to the King. They replied by stating that the purpose for which they had come was to induce the King of England forthwith to abandon his project of the conquest of Cyprus, and to hurry over to Acre with all his forces. The allied chiefs of the Christians were impatient of further delay, and the King of France had declared that he would do nothing more, as the English reinforcements were not forthcoming. They also accused the King of England of attacking and murdering fellow Christians, whilst the Saracens whom he had undertaken to fight with were over-running the Holy Land unchecked. Their accusations were of so violent a character that the King was enraged, and replied in a manner and with such oaths and violence, as to render their embassy and arguments of little effect. The bishop and his companion regretfully withdrew from the royal audience, carrying back with them to Acre an unsatisfactory report of the intentions of the English King.[1]

[1] Vinsauf, II. 37.

AN ENGLISH KING. 121

This incident is of interest as showing how divided the views of the Crusaders appear to have been in the mattter of the occupation of Cyprus. The political breach which existed between the French and their Anglo-Norman allies was clearly enough defined from the very outset of the expedition from Lyons—and such an incident as the occupation of Cyprus served to increase the international animosity. The French doubtless felt that the strong influence which their ancestors under Godfrey de Bouillon had established in the Levantine principalities, would be seriously prejudiced by an English foothold of so important a character in the very centre of the Levant.

Dismissing the ambassadors, with all their adverse criticism of his projects, from his presence and his mind, King Richard turned with his usual energy to the prosecution of his present enterprise in Cyprus—an enterprise which met with the highest approval of most of his contemporaries and with eulogium in after years by those who wrote the chronicles of his deeds, and his epitaph at Fontevrault.

As Master Geoffrey the Cellarer saw him standing on the beach of Constantia, in all the pride of manhood, in the flower of his age, he was not the type of soldier to abandon a project once formed. He had decided that Cyprus should form the impregnable bulwark of Christendom—which it did for more than three centuries after his time—whatever happened to Jerusalem and Acre, and he was not to be frightened or cajoled from his course of action by the King of France or his emissary the Bishop of Beauvais.

On the departure of the unwelcome envoys from Acre, orders were issued to the Crusaders to be in readiness at daybreak on the morrow for the march into the interior of the island.

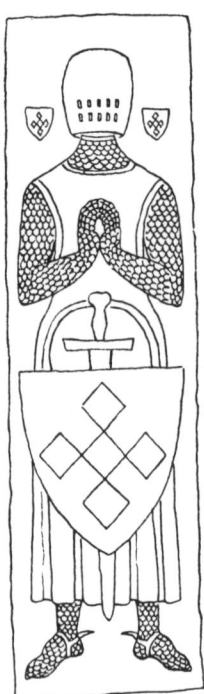

Tombstone of unknown knight found in Nicosia, 1880.

CHAPTER XI.

AT daybreak on the following morning, amidst the brilliance of an eastern dawn, the army of the Crusaders began its march into the Messaoria of Cyprus. The dark forms of the men-at-arms in their leathern jerkins, shouldering pikes and battle-axes, were a sombre setting to the knights on horseback, clad in the sinuous chain mail which glittered with every movement of the wearer like the scales of a snake, in the early morning sunshine.

The knights and their followers had been cautioned that the district they would pass through would be deserted, and that food was consequently difficult to procure, every man therefore was provided with a bag of rations and some sort of pilgrims bottle wherein to carry wine sufficient for a day or two.

AN ENGLISH KING. 123

The path followed by the army after quitting Constantia and its suburb of Encomi, where the numerous tombs of the ancients constituted a sort of Appian Way leading from the site of ancient Salamis, was for some distance the same road along which the army of King Guy had approached Constantia from Amathus. But the perfectly flat plain of the Messaoria in the centre of the island admitted of many wandering tracks and more or less practicable roads in summer time. In winter immense morasses and marshes impeded all means of communication, and the deep alluvial mud of the river Pediæs and other streams had, with difficulty, to be avoided.

At the villages of Kouklia and Kalopsyda the road turned off to the north-west and the country became broken up with cañons formed by winter torrents, which had deeply cut their ways into the soft alluvial soil, which afforded cover and protection for an ambuscade where trees and woodland were nowhere to be found. The Messaoria, its vast expanse dotted here and there with mud-built villages, was only covered with low bushes of shinia and clumps of asphodel, wherever an occasional patch of cultivated land had not encroached upon the wilderness.

Already the Crusaders had experienced the fighting tactics of the natives. As they were crossing a very deep river bed, and a large body of them were in the hollow, they were surprised by a flight of arrows striking them in a very unexpected manner from the direction of the streamlet. The enemy was in fact concealed by a bend in the steep sides of the cañon at some distance higher up ; by the time they had recovered from the surprise and disorder occasioned by this attack and had despatched some men-at-arms and crossbowmen to take vengeance on their foes, the enemy had decamped.

The one or two men wounded in this crafty manner having been attended to by some serving brothers of the hospital, the army continued its march, but with greater precautions. On more than one occasion they found this attempt to harass them repeated by bodies of the enemy who, lurking in the river beds, were able to conceal themselves very effectually, and did not attempt hostilities in the open, or where the roads passed over the higher levels of the plain.

At length the brown mud buildings of a somewhat important village came into view ; the Crusaders were informed that this was Tremythus where the Despot had collected his forces, and where he would probably give them battle. Rejoiced at the prospect of a decisive engagement with the enemy, the Crusaders approached the village in as good order as the nature of the ground permitted. In advance were several knights mounted on their chargers and each surrounded by his " clump of spears"; these were supported by the crossbowmen and other men-at-arms, whilst the rear was brought up by King Richard and a number of knights and lords of high degree. The red cross banner of the King and the pennons of the feudatories gave a certain vivacity to the scene.

As the army was pressing on to the village with enthusiasm, and the terrible battle cry of " Dex Aie " was occasionally taken up in chorus by the advancing warriors, a skirmish with some of the enemy arbalesters denoted that a battle was imminent, and that the hopes of the Anglo-Normans would not be disappointed. At the same time the presence of the main force of the Despot's army was evidenced by a body of seven hundred stradiotes or cavalry making a charge against the right flank of the Crusaders. In both cases the enemy was successfully driven off. More native levies now appeared upon the scene and a considerable battle was taking place. The Despot, who now appeared, was no coward in warfare and displayed astonishing activity in marshalling and encouraging his troops. He even attempted to draw King Richard into a personal combat, but in the traditional Parthian manner he wished to kill the English King with poisoned arrows, which fortunately did not hit their mark, and when Cœur de Lion tried to strike him with his lance he eluded the blow in a very dexterous manner. But soon the issue of the battle was the complete victory of the Anglo-Norman invaders, and the two Kings Richard and Guy were consulting how their forces should be recalled from a desultory pursuit of their foes.

The Despot had fled before the conclusion of the fighting, to the northern range of hills, where, on a romantic rock, stood the castle of Cantara. This castle, of which the mediæval ruins of a later period than the twelfth century are still wonderfully preserved, was in those days an

AN ENGLISH KING. 125

equally impregnable fortress. But the forces of the Despot were dispersed : his rule had been that of an avaricious tyrant, and he had been an usurper of the worst description ; the more conservative amongst the natives— and the Byzantines were a very conservative race—viewed him with detestation as an upstart of the imperial house who had usurped the position of their Orthodox emperor.

The career of the self-styled " Emperor of Cyprus " was at an end. The Anglo-Normans under the English King were in possession of the island, and any resistance, still maintained in the more remote parts, could be overcome without difficulty.

The battlefield of Tremythus, or Tremethousha, on which the fate of Cyprus was decided seven hundred and thirty-five years ago, may still be recognised beneath its modern veil of peaceful industry, its far-reaching fields of corn and barley, its encircling villages with their softly outlined mud-built houses, and their vast threshing floors.

It was the beginning of midsummer, when the villager of the plain gathers the vast cereal wealth of surrounding fields into mountainous stacks, and then sets to work slowly and gradually to thresh out the corn on the open earth floor in a manner truly primitive and patriarchal.

Battlefield of Tremythus, and church of St. Spyridon.

The Anglo-Norman strangers noticed with curiosity the abandoned agricultural implements lying on the threshing floors—implements unlike any they were accustomed to in Europe. The δουκάναις, or tribula, a curious substitute for the flail in a country where there are no barns, which consists of two very heavy planks of wood framed together forming a kind of sledge, studded underneath with small sharp pieces of flint, to be dragged around the corn heap in a circular way by oxen, mules, and donkeys. When the broken-up straw is cleared away, the corn remains to be winnowed in the evening breeze with wooden shovels and, collected into heaps, becomes the farmers' wealth, and the staple on which the whole community relies for its existence during the year.

In the stir and turmoil of an invasion of Cyprus, not only would all the business of life be suspended, but the villagers not forced to enlist in the army of the Despot would fly to the hills, and the brown mud-walled villages of the Messaoria were comparatively deserted when the Norman Crusaders penetrated into their midst.

After the victory, King Richard and his army are said to have marched to Nicosia (or Ledra as the village was then named). But in the ancient town-lists of Cyprus there is neither the name of Nicosia nor Ledra, and the principal town of the Messaoria is always Trimythos.[1] Probably Trimythos having been plundered and partly burnt in the fashion of the times would serve as a resting place for the Normans, and here King Richard seems to have had one of his frequent sicknesses.

In Tremythus stood—probably much as it stands to-day— an ancient church and monastery of St. Spyridon ; a venerable looking double-naved building containing the small Byzantine sarcophagus of the famous holy man, whose relics were carried off to Corfu in 1460, and there became a source of much miracle-mongering in a later age. After the battle this venerable building was thronged with the devout Crusaders prostrating themselves before the tomb which now stands empty and neglected beneath the ruins of an ancient eiconostasion within the southern nave.

At the time of the Anglo-Norman occupation the central parts of the island—the great Messaoria plain— was the only portion, in addition to the sea coast, brought under European influence and government. The mountain districts were of too savage and poor a description to admit of much control, they in fact seem to have been considered negligible until almost the English occupation in 1878. In the Bronze Age the centre of population was in the neighbourhood of Kythrea (the Chytroi of the ancients) and along the course of the river Pediæs. The Egyptians,

[1] Hackett p. 242.

AN ENGLISH KING. 127

Phœnicians, Greeks and Romans had formed their colonies on the seashore on different sides of the island, but the Byzantines, influenced by the spread of Christianity incorporated themselves more thoroughly with the aborigines, in the interior, and Tremythus seems to have been the episcopal centre of the Messaoria.

The battle of Tremythus having definitely settled the fate of the island, the army of occupation established itself in the village as a base of operations and general headquarters, whilst a body of men-at-arms and knights was dispatched to secure the only important castle remaining in the hands of the natives which was situated at Kyrenia.

The small seaport of Kyrenia was of a certain importance in Byzantine times, but its inhabitants were very willing to exchange their allegiance to the Despot for a much more civilised form of government such as the Europeans offered them, they were therefore in readiness to welcome King Guy and his attendant knights when they appeared before the gate of the small town. As the Normans rode down the gorge of Agirda to take possession of this part of the island, the singular resemblance of the scenery to that of the Italian coast near Messina impressed everyone. At the bottom of the gorge lay the little town of Kyrenia backed in the view by the dark blue sea, whilst far off on the horizon was the long range of the Taurus mountains on the opposite coast closing one of the most beautiful prospects in the world, whilst to east and west stretched the forest clad slopes of the northern hills of Cyprus.

The Despot finding himself abandoned by his subjects, and more especially by the Orthodox clergy, was within a few days obliged to throw himself upon the mercy of King Richard. He came down from the northern hills, and having obtained an audience of the King, approached the royal tent with due expression of humility and resignation. As he entered the royal presence he flung himself on the ground at the feet of the King in the eastern manner of a servant approaching an offended master. The King ordered him to rise through his interpreter, and then directed that he should be seated for an interview.

The Despot's surrender was made on the terms that he should not be subjected to the indignity and misery of being fettered or placed in irons. This the English King conceded together with his life, but as the metal of the bonds with which he could be confined had been specified as iron, and nothing had been said about silver he was obliged to submit to chains of that precious metal with which his movements were impeded and his abject condition as a prisoner was enforced. He was then confided to the charge of Ralph the Chamberlain.

The Despot had a daughter, to whom he was particularly attached, who at the time of the Crusaders' invasion was resident in Kyrenia. This daughter was handed over as a prisoner to King Guy on his occupation of the northern stronghold, and in due course was brought to the camp in the middle of the island. Here she found her father a prisoner, and an affecting meeting took place between parent and child and also a parting, for the Despot, condemned to imprisonment for life, had been handed over to the Hospitallers for safe keeping, and was about to leave Cyprus for ever on board one of their galleys for their castle at Margat in Syria.

The young Comnenian princess was sent to Amathus to the care of the newly crowned Queen of England.

The day at length was dawning which was to see the Kings of England and Jerusalem, with the greater part of their followers depart from Cyprus, on the quest of still greater adventures in the Holy Land.

Overnight the last meetings of the council had been held to discuss all the multifarious details of European occupation which had been established in so short a time. The appointment of functionaries, the general procedure for taxation and revenue, and the maintenance of certain local organizations had afforded much occupation. Two English barons were to remain as justiciaries in the name of the King of England and to be responsible for the administration of law and order. A comparatively small body of knights and men-at-arms was to be left behind to act as garrison for the principal castles. These arrangements were considered sufficient under the circumstances, as the attitude of the natives seemed evidently conciliatory towards the new government and its administrators. The names of Richard de Camville and Robert de Turnham are recorded as those of the two men to whom Cœur de Lion confided the care of his new possession, the latter was in all probability a brother of the more famous Stephen de Turnham, Richard's favourite in his Palestine campaigns.

AN ENGLISH KING. 129

The cries of the sailors, the notes of horns and trumpets, and all the sounds of departure were resounding in Salamis bay, as the sun began to mount the heavens on this eventful morn. The horses had been once more consigned to the holds of the transports, and the port holes through which they had been passed had been caulked again. Certain of the ships had been loaded with plunder, for the departing knights and men-at-arms could not be expected to leave a country where they had been treated with much enmity and illwill, without exacting certain booty in compensation. The two kings had also received much " backshish " from their new subjects, and the treasures of the ex-Despot which had been seized in Kyrenia were considerable ; the fleet riding in Salamis bay was in fact laden with spoil.

With swelling sails and fluttering streamers the great English transports were one by one hauling in their anchors, and beginning to steer on a south-easterly course for Acre. The lighter galleys and rowboats were following the great ships, their rowers plying their oars in leisurely fashion, as the royal galley was one of the last to move from its moorings.

King Richard stood on the poop for the last time surveying the island realm, which he had won with so much ease, and yet with a certain éclat. The flat levels of the Salamis shore stretched away for miles on either hand to north and south, and with a sense of immeasurable distance the plain of Messaoria formed its own horizon. The far distant purple mountains ministered to the imposing effect of a vast distance. In the foreground lay the insignificant looking town of Constantia with its curious aqueduct disappearing in countless arches across the plain. Some few old Roman columns still stood upon their bases giving an air of ruined magnificence to the scene in the early morning light.

As King Richard leant against the stern gunwale of his galley, his speculative mind was filled with singular musings on the strange events of the past six weeks in which he had played the leading part. Before him lay stretched the full breadth of this fair possession in the very centre of the then known world : but how long could it be retained as an appanage of the English crown ? obviously it was too far away ; and as obviously it was designed by Divine Providence to become the main support for a restored Latin Kingdom of Jerusalem. King Richard soon turned away from the sunlit landscape and these problems with a furrowed brow, and the practical conclusion that such a prize as Cyprus would always fetch a high price, and with this his attention became rivetted on his quickly sailing fleet, the flashing oars of the rowers, and the first sight of the distant mountains of the Holy Land.

AN ENGLISH KING. 131

Latin families in Cyprus.
1. De Nores.   2. Visconti.   3. Tabarie.
4. Neville.   5. Milmars.   6. Neville.
7. Nefin.   8. Milmars.   9. Prevost.

CHAPTER XII.

KING Richard proceeded on his way eastwards, leaving Cyprus on the 1st June, 1191, arriving at Acre on the 8th of the same month after having visited Tyre and Tripoli en route.

For about six months the Anglo-Norman occupation of Cyprus continued without serious difficulty or disturbance; The Cypriots were at first satisfied to exchange the tyranny of the Despot, although he was of their own kindred and mode of thought, for a foreign domination and the imposition of the European feudal law, but with the lessening number of the English men-at-arms and their camp followers, as they were drawn away by the exigencies of the campaign in Palestine, a spirit of revolt began to spread amongst the villages, and the collection of taxation was rendered difficult. The death of Richard de Camville was also a misfortune, throwing all the responsibility of government on to Robert de Turnham, a man who was perhaps better qualified to act as a seaman and admiral.

Towards the end of the year 1191, a rising of the villagers in the mountain districts, where the natives disaffected towards the foreign invasion had found a refuge, was set on foot. A monk said to be some relative of the deposed Despot was proclaimed Emperor of Cyprus, and his supporters proceeded to attack the representatives of the foreign administration. Robert de Turnham was however equal to the occasion and quickly marching upon the rebels before they had matured their plans, captured the emperor-elect and promptly hanged him on the nearest tree.

News of the revolt and disaffection of the Cypriots soon reached King Richard at Acre. He began to realize the difficulties in the tenancy of this rich and much coveted island, by a foreign power so far away as the Normandy of that period. He evidently wished to keep it in reserve as a refuge for the Latins in event of that collapse which occurred almost exactly a century later, which he seems to have foreseen and provided for, but meanwhile his political schemes were complicated by a variety of peculiar circumstances.

In the first and foremost place there was the prospect of a recovered kingdom of Jerusalem, of which it is evident that Cœur de Lion proposed to become a very important patron if not the suzerain. Towards this project the possession of Cyprus would have been an important stepping stone, if the scheme had ever matured. But the crown of Jerusalem was a prize coveted by several claimants. As already mentioned in referring to the history of Guy de Lusignan, the succession to the throne was complicated by the presence of two heiresses, who as it were, became the pawns in a political game of genealogical chances. These unhappy ladies, Sibylla and Isabella, had no less than six husbands between them, two of whom were patronised by Richard Cœur de Lion. But Richard's patronage of Sibylla's husband Guy de Lusignan, seems to have somewhat waned when his nephew Count Henry of Champagne was enabled to marry Isabella, after her husband Conrad de Montferrat had been murdered on April 27th, 1192. Political schemes and projects were of the most tortuous and varied character at this period, and it is difficult to realize the motives governing the actions

AN ENGLISH KING. 133

of the Lionhearted king during his stay in Palestine when political events were changing and succeeding each other rapidly.

Meanwhile the exigencies of the campaign and the inevitable want of money induced Richard I., as suzerain of Cyprus, to entertain a project which had been laid before him to pass the island over to the Order of the Temple, as a sort of speculation.

The famous Order of the Temple, or of the " poor knights of Jesus Christ " which played so important a rôle in the history of the Latin kingdom, and incidentally in the occupation of Cyprus, must be described, as far as its scanty records permit. It was founded about the year 1120 as a purely military organization, or " legion " as we should call it at the present day, for the purpose of protecting the passage of the pilgrims to the Holy Land, and the possessions of the Frank settlers.

The convents of the Order were usually fortified when built in Europe, as for instance the famous Commanderies of Paris and London, and innumerable smaller granges or preceptories; in the Levant immense fortresses were the equivalents of the abbeys of the Benedictines, Carmelites, or Augustinians. The principal fortresses of the Order in Palestine and Syria were the magnificent Haram enclosure at Jerusalem, Athlit, near Haifa, and Tortosa, in the north. Acre was also a headquarters of the Templar marine. This district comprised fourteen commanderies, to which must be added those of Armenia and Cyprus. Some architectural peculiarities in the method of fortification are noticeable, distinguishing the Templar castles from others of the same period.

The conception of a military confraternity was hardly an original idea on the part of the French knight Hugh de Payen at the beginning of the twelfth century. Similar confraternities have always been and will always be associated with standing armies. But certain aspects of its organization due to religious and social conditions of the period constitute a great difference between this and similar institutions.

St. Bernard of Clairvaux was perhaps more truly the chief founder of the Order. He induced the Pope Honorius II. to patronize it, and to him is due the " Rule " or constitution of its laws drawn up at the council of Troyes in

January, 1128. This "Rule" in its original form was unfortunately destroyed when the Order was abolished in 1312, but copies of the later Rules still survive.[1] The Templars took the three evangelical vows of chastity, obedience, and poverty living together as canons regular, and sharing the dormitory, refectory, and offices of a conventual establishment, the Rule being modelled on that of the Cistercians.

Like any other religious Order of the middle ages, that of the Temple was divided into the two classes of superiors, or knights, and inferiors, or serving brothers. Amongst the upper class were the chaplains, and only such members as could prove their gentle birth; for a serving brother, or sergeant, it was sufficient that he was not base-born. In both classes members could be admitted on agreement terminable under certain conditions, but the majority were probably under vows for life : King Fulk of Jerusalem is said to have been a member of the Order before his coronation.

St. Bernard's description of a Templar knight is singularly graphic : "They live together without separate property, in one house under one rule, careful to preserve the unity of the spirit in the bond of peace......Draughts and dice they detest ; hunting they hold in abomination ....songs and stage plays they eschew as insane follies. They cut close the hair, knowing as the Apostle says, that " it is a shame for a man to have long hair." They never dress gaily, and wash but seldom. Shaggy by reason of their uncombed hair, they are also begrimed with dust, and swarthy from the weight of their armour and the heat of the sun."

The great officers of the Order : the Grand Master, Seneschal, Marshal, and the Grand Commanders of particular districts or provinces, had a considerable retinue in attendance upon them. Each knight like a feudal seigneur was the captain of a levy of men-at-arms and was under the control of his district commander. In addition there were large bodies of native mercenaries in the Levant under the command of officers called "Turcopoliers." The knights, although professed as celibate monks or friars, were attended by their esquires in the same way as feudal lords.

[1] The Order is said to have been reformed in Portugal as the "Order of Christ."

AN ENGLISH KING. 135

The dress of the knights was regulated by the Pope at their first institution. It consisted of a white linen surcoat marked with a full red cross; the squires and sergeants wore brown leather jerkins or black linen surcoats, also marked with the great red cross.

The standard of the Templars was the famous "Beauseant," a flag parted black and white, intended to signify that the Order was black and drear to the enemies of the Christian religion but fair and favourable to its friends. These outward symbols of the "Religion" remained unchanged during the two centuries of its existence.

Matthew of Paris states that the Templars owned about 70,000 manors in western Christendom comprising preceptories or schools for recruiting purposes and homes for aged knights and servants.

Many Templars attained exalted positions in the state, such as the Grand Almoner of England in Henry III.'s time, but they were not allowed to become members of other Orders.

The peculiar social position of the Order, in its vast wealth, and its feudal possessions gave it the opportunity of becoming a powerful commercial corporation, and this was one of the chief reasons of its unpopularity in France and Italy. In peace time it controlled much of the Levantine commerce, and in war, under the pretext of protecting it, committed acts of the most shameless avarice combined with treachery.

The trading ships and war-galleys of the Order formed a very powerful navy in the Mediterranean, with agents, stores, and arsenals in every important port of the Levant. In each of the Commanderies the control of the fortress was in the hands of the "Conventual Bailiffs," *i.e.*, the Grand Commander, the Treasurer, and the Turcopolier.

The Templars were always on the most friendly terms with the English and the Anglo-Normans of the twelfth century. This was due to an absence of that commercial rivalry which influenced their relations with the Italian and French trading communities of the Mediterranean. Richard Cœur de Lion is said to have appeared in the garb of a Templar on certain occasions, in any case the most distinguishing badge of the Order and of the English Crusaders happens to have been identical.

Owing to the complete loss of all the chartularies and other documents connected with the Order, we are unable to do more than surmise what the arrangements may have been between the new suzerain lord of Cyprus and the council of the Temple when the island was handed over as a fief of the Anglo-Norman crown. The price to be paid for it is stated to have been 100,000 bezants d'or, equivalent, according to Mas Latrie (1860) to about eight millions of francs.[1] The gold besant was usually styled *bezant sarrasin*, because the money coined by Christian princes was invariably of silver. An immediate payment of 40,000 gold pieces was made by the Templars to King Richard and the remainder were guaranteed by the pledge or mortgage of one of the castles belonging to the Order in North Syria.[2]

In his "Tresor de Chronologie," Mas Latrie states that the Grand Mastership of the Order was vacant in 1191, but in his "Histoire de Chypre" I., p. 29, he describes how the affair of the sale of Cyprus took place before the 13th July, the day on which Acre was captured by the combined forces of the French and Anglo-Normans. He also states that Robert de Sablé, afterwards Grand Master, one of the Seigneurs of Maine, came to the east with King Richard, and was probably the purchaser.

With all due regard for the learned Mas Latrie's profound knowledge of these events it seems more than probable that this transaction of the sale of the island must have taken place some time after the fall of Acre. More than a month must surely have elapsed during which the difficulties in administration were to develop, a rising of disaffected natives was to be put down, and all the necessary negotiations over a purchase and sale of eight millions of francs worth of property could be concluded. It is therefore more probable that the Templars had not obtained possession of the island until well into the autumn —perhaps Christmas—of 1191.

From what subsequently occurred it would seem that the Templars immediately set about building one of their fortified towers in the centre of the island at a village then known as Ledra, but afterwards called "Nicosia." Here they probably planned a block-house fort very much

---

[1] M. Latrie "Histoire" p. 29.   [2] Cont. Will. Tyre, p. 189.

like the still surviving Colossi castle near Limassol, which although of the fifteenth century, is built on the model of five hundred years before. According to the chronicler Amadi, the 60,000 bezants were regarded in the nature of a loan on mortgage, the interest on which was paid out of the revenue of the island.[1] The Templars had been in the custom of investing their money in derelict estates and manoirs in the Holy Land and elsewhere. More especially was this the case in the thirteenth century, when many of the original settlers, or their descendants, conscious of the uncertainty of holding such estates and fiefs exposed to the endless warfare of the Levant, sold them to the great Orders and abandoned the country.[2] Hence the idea of purchasing the feudal rights over Cyprus would be proposed and accepted by the Templars as a very feasable thing to do under the circumstances of the inevitably impecunious condition of the Anglo-Norman Crusaders at that time besieging Acre.

During the months of July and August 1191, a great council or parliament of seigneurs and prelates was held at St. Jean d'Acre, at which very important matters connected with the prosecution of the Crusade, and also the settlement of the Latin Kingdom were agreed upon. It was settled that Guy de Lusignan should be regarded as a life tenant of the kingdom, but without right of succession to any of his possible heirs in case of his re-marriage, and that Conrad of Montferrat and his wife Isabella and their descendants should be recognised as heirs to the kingdom on his death.[3]

Shortly after the meeting of this council, the King of France who had been ill for some time took his departure from Acre with his household, but the greater part of his forces remained behind and continued under the Duke of Burgundy to co-operate with the Anglo-Normans.[4] King Richard leaving Acre proceeded southwards on his famous campaign in 1192—that unfortunate fruitless effort to recover the Holy City which seemed so near accomplishment, and yet became so purposeless. On the 23rd of August, Richard was able to leave behind him the re-established and consolidated capital of what amounted

[1] Amadi, p. 83. [2] C. L. Kingsford: "Crusades" p. 177.
[3] Mas Latrie, Histoire, I. 30. [4] Mas Latrie, Histoire, Ibid.

to a new Latin Kingdom, of which Cyprus was soon to become the most important part. Guy de Lusignan accompanied the King of England and took part in the battles on the famous coast march, at the head of a Poitevin contingent. The council of the Templars considered it sufficient to send a very small body of knights and men-at-arms into the island to take possession of their new acquisition. This—as it proved—very inadequate force, was under the command of Ser Arnaut Bouchart.[1]

Cyprus was regarded by its new proprietors much as a colony in modern days would be by a commercial or chartered company, to be held chiefly as a source of revenue for the benefit of the shareholders, the only difference being that the Templars treated the natives in a harsh injudicious manner which would be impossible under modern conditions. Not content with land and poll taxes, they exacted high tariffs on all merchandise, payable not only by the vendor but also by the buyer.[2] These extortions were more especially resented by the merchants of the port towns, and perhaps by the Europeans settled in such places, who found their trade hampered and paralysed by such a system.

For three or four months the Commander Ser Arnaut Bouchart with his assistants, endeavoured to continue the Latin occupation of Cyprus in conformity with the European feudal law, but in the early spring of the year 1192 the discontented natives recovering from that apathetic subjection to which they had been reduced by the rapid and overwhelming progress of King Richard's conquest of the island, once more attempted to shake off the foreign despotism which had been imposed upon them.[3] The nationalist elements in the population, which had given rise to the insurrection so promptly terminated by Robert de Turnham a few months before, had once more come to a head, and a conspiracy was formed for the purpose of exterminating the whole body of Europeans then established in the centre of the island. At this date (beginning of 1192) we begin to hear for the first time of "Nicosia," as the capital ; this name appears to have supplanted the older one of " Ledra " or " Lefkosia "

[1] Contin, Will. Tyre, 190. [2] Chron. d'Amadi, 9.
[3] M. Latrie, I., 33.

AN ENGLISH KING. 139

attaching to one of the older villages in the centre of the Messaoria, and of which the actual site seems to have changed at different periods. The modern Nicosia which was established in the twelfth century as the island capital is surrounded by sites of ruined villages covered with debris, or marked by ancient cemeteries, any one of which may have been its predecessor under the name of Ledra. Here the castle referred to in the chronicles—already described above as a sort of blockhouse fort—was now partly built in the centre of the village, and its presence evidently excited the native animosity and the idea that if it was completed the chances of ever recovering a national independence would be small indeed.

The works at the new castle were defended by stockades and a formidable ditch through which the river had been conducted; the position of the foreign invaders was becoming impregnable if they could complete their castle without disturbance.

Around this monument of a new and tyrannous government, the mutinous peasants, instigated by the townsfolk from the ports, were collected with evidently hostile intentions, and expressions of hatred and defiance.[1]

The plot to massacre the Latins in their new fortification of Nicosia was brought to a head by the beginning of April, 1192, and Holy Saturday before Easter was selected as the day when a large number of peasants would be assembled for the Easter fair or panegiri, and their presence would be of assistance.

The oriental and Latin Easters happened to coincide in the year 1192, and the festival fell upon the 5th April.[2]

The chronicler Amadi gives an elaborate account of this tragedy which ended in terrible bloodshed and misfortune for the Cypriots.

"In the times when the Templars held Cyprus, the Greeks, exasperated by an imposition of a tax for holding their Saturday market, thought to attack and kill all the Latins. Fra Arnaud Bochard who was Grand Commander of Cyprus, hearing of this, called together all the Latins that he could find, and put them within the castle at Nicosia, which was then but a feeble fortification, afterwards rebuilt and strengthened by King Guy. Those who entered within the castle, numbered fourteen knights,

[1] M. Latrie, "Histoire" I., 33.   [2] M. Latrie, ibid.

seventy-four men-at-arms, and twenty-nine other horsemen, (Turcoples ?), but they were without victuals and they were filled with forebodings. They ventured to demand of the Greeks a free passage, and to be allowed to abandon the country : but they received a reply that they would all be killed to avenge the deaths of such of the natives as had died at the hands of the Latins. Arnaud Bochard on hearing this, addressed the others, saying : " Sirs, you see the vindictiveness of these people, and the evil they design against you, therefore I vote that we fight with them as valiant men, instead of dying of hunger, here within, like cowards." To these words they all agreed, and the following day, at dawn, having first heard Mass, they issued out of the castle on a sudden, and began slaying the Greeks who were taken off their guard, and could not believe that so small a party of men would undertake such an enterprise. So not being in any order, the villagers were completely routed, and the Latins chased them through the lanes (of Nicosia) and killed as many as they could find. And a number of persons having taken refuge in a church, the Latins entered into the church and killed them all. Some of the Templars provided themselves with spears in a crossed form attached to the saddle-bow and in this way killed and wounded many. The killing and hewing off limbs was so great, that the blood ran down into the river, from the bridge of the Seneschal to the bridge of the Berline, where is now placed a great stone as a memorial of this affair.

The Templars then went through the land, sacking, and taking all that they could find, and were able to consider themselves safe and in quiet. The villagers fled for fear of them into the mountains and the farms became deserted, on which account the Templars seeing that they would not be able to derive any profit from the land, were minded to hold a council for deciding how the island should be guarded, and also how the debt of 60,000 ducats was to be paid to the King of England."[1]

At the moment when these tragic events were taking place in the centre of Cyprus, King Richard was at Ascalon, immersed in the troubles consequent upon the desertion of the Crusade by the important French contingent, by the reassembling of the Saracens under Saladin, and by

[1] Chron. d'Amadi, p. 84.

AN ENGLISH KING.   141

the still more important difficulties occasioned by the fratricidal quarrels between the Genoese and Pisans supporting rival claimants to the throne of the Latin Kingdom.

Conrad, Marquess of Montferrat, has already been referred to in giving some account of the Kingdom of Jerusalem. As a daring Italian adventurer he had secured a very great following in Palestine and Syria, and all those who foresaw the ultimate fate of the Holy Land, and were not much influenced by what we should call at the present time a "legitimist sentiment" were ready to abandon the cause of Guy de Lusignan the truly anointed King of Jerusalem for this bold unscrupulous pretender.

Master Geoffrey the Cellarer had accompanied the crusading army first to Acre, and then on the march towards the south. He was evidently keenly observant of King Richard's somewhat changeable policy at this juncture of affairs : we cannot have a better view of the course of events than through his record and diary.[1]

King Richard continued to recognize Guy de Lusignan as the legitimate King, but he also recognised his want of suitable qualifications for so difficult a post—in other words his inferiority. It had been settled at Acre that Guy should remain a mere life-tenant in any case, and this no doubt had much to do with the opinions of all interested in the matter. It is of interest to find that King Richard was regarded so much in the light of "King-maker," and his consent and approval of anything like an election to the crown seems to have been of the utmost importance. For some little time Richard continued to weigh the advantages to be gained either by espousing the cause of the Italian, who was also the protegée of the French, or of continuing to support his own vassal the Norman prince who was de facto King of Jerusalem.

[1] It. Regis Angl., Book V.

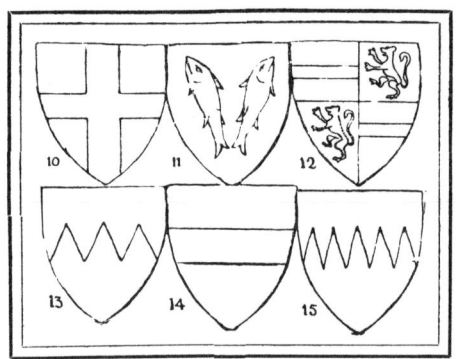

Latin families in Cyprus.
10. Angulier. 11. Dampierre. 12. Thenouri.
13, 15. Moustri. 14. Tabarie, and Lambert.

CHAPTER XIII.

MEANWHILE the departing French—700 knights and a proportionate number of men-at-arms—under the Duke of Burgundy, had reached Tyre where they were to find their shipping. Here, resigning all thoughts of the Crusade and giving themselves up to the grossest luxury and debauchery, they exhibited the extraordinary contrasts which were common in the days of the Crusades : on one side religious fanaticism and aceticism, on the other profligacy and licence of the worst description. At Tyre they were entertained by the Marquess Conrad, whom they were most ready to support in his claims and pretensions.

The sea-faring season being once more open, one of the first persons to arrive from England with most important news for King Richard was the Prior of Hereford who had been sent by the Chancellor, William de Longchamp, on this special mission. He informed the king of the acts of his brother John, who had seized the government of the kingdom, and the castles, and all the yearly revenue in the Exchequer. " If " said the Prior " the king does not take speedy counsel in these matters, and return

AN ENGLISH KING. 143

home in all haste and avenge his wrongs on the insurgents, it will fare worse, and he will not be able to recover his kingdom without the hazard of war."

The King was astounded at the news, and troubled beyond measure with the difficulties in front of him, for he knew that if he were obliged to return home on a sudden, as there was so much strife and jealousy between the people of Tyre and Ascalon, without doubt the Saracens would be able to gain possession of the Holy Land and retain it for ever.

On the morrow of the Prior of Hereford's arrival, the King called together the leaders of the Crusaders and laid before them this news about his kingdom of England, declaring that it was necessary for him to return home immediately, but offering at the same time to leave behind him a contingent of 300 knights and 2,000 chosen men-at-arms, at his own expense. He then enquired who would return with him, and who would stay behind?

At the council of Ascalon some weighty matters were discussed seriously affecting the future of the Holy Land and incidentally the fate of Cyprus. King Richard had asked the opinion of those present as to the settlement of the Latin Kingdom of Jerusalem. In reply the general sentiment was expressed that in view of so much discord amongst different parties, and the uncertainty of events, and especially as King Guy had failed in effecting the recovery of his kingdom, it became necessary that a new king should be appointed to whom all could pay allegiance. Also it was intimated that if this were not done, the Crusaders, one and all, would be obliged to depart from a land which it would be impossible to guard, without a duly appointed king. On this King Richard demanded which would be the king they would rather have : the Norman Guy, or the Italian Conrad. The representatives of the army, high and low, then declared that the Marquess of Montferrat should be elevated to the dignity as the best man that they could choose for the purpose of defending the country. King [Richard thereupon felt bound to censure the assembled knights for their fickleness, for they had before this often detracted from the good qualities of the Marquess, whom they now professed to regard as so great a man. As a result of this council, a galley was despatched to Tyre from Ascalon, having on board Henry, Count of Champagne, Richard's nephew, Odo de Transinges, and William de Cagne, with a retinue, to acquaint the Marquess Conrad with his election.

Master Geoffrey's opinion of the Marquess was anything but satisfactory and this opinion was shared by many others. There were rumours of his plots against the King of England, and of his secret treaties with the Saracens, of his intentions to sacrifice the interests of all the Crusaders for the purpose of securing to himself the half of the Holy Land, whilst the other half he proposed abandoning to the Egyptian Sultan. But the truth of these reports of his bad faith has never been confirmed for he was prematurely cut off almost at the very moment of his receiving the news of his election.

The ambassadors from Ascalon had been warmly welcomed, the people of Tyre hailed with enthusiasm the prospect of their prince becoming King of Jerusalem, and the most elaborate preparations for a suitable celebration of his coronation were set on foot. But hardly had Count Henry of Champagne and his companions boarded their galley once more to set sail for Acre, where they proposed paying a visit on their way back to Ascalon, when the catastrophe occurred which plunged every one into mourning and despair.

The Marquess Conrad, after bidding adieu to the Norman embassy, had paid a visit to his old supporter and adherent the Bishop of Beauvais where he was entertained at dinner. On leaving the Bishop's hostel, he mounted his horse to ride home to his palace by the sea, but as he passed the custom house, two young men approached him with a letter which they offered him. He accepted this, and was about to read it, when with a sudden dexterity the young men drew their daggers, and stabbed him to the heart, immediately running off at full speed. One of the murderers was captured and killed on the spot; the other escaped to a church, but was dragged thence and tortured into the confession that the instigator of the deed was "the old man of the Mountain," or chief of the fraternity of the assassins or "hashish" votaries.

The sect of Mohammedans known as the "Assassins" or "Hashishians" (votaries of a drug derived from hemp,

AN ENGLISH KING. 145

or "hashish") were also known as the Ismailians or followers of Ismail the sixth Imam. They are supposed by some to have been the predecessors of the modern Druses—but fanatical sects of dervishes all bear a certain resemblance to each other. The extraordinary training in obedience, secrecy, and self-devotion, of the young men of the sect has rarely been equalled, and never been surpassed by any secret society of fanatics, and gave rise to many strange legends in the middle ages.

In the twelfth century the assassins formed a powerful community or clan in the Lebanon mountains under a sheik or chieftain called the "Old Man"; they even possessed fortresses and controlled the trade of their district, evidently owning no allegiance to the Latin princes of Tripoli and Antioch.

The assassination of the Marquess of Montferrat was attributed at the time, and with great probability, to the "Old Man of the Mountain" who desired to avenge certain acts of piracy and robbery committed by the Latins on some merchant ships visiting the Lebanon coast.

On receiving his deadly wounds, the Marquess fell from his horse, rolling on the ground in mortal agony. The spectators ran to raise him and carry him to the palace, and his wife, summoned in haste, was just able to receive his last commands before he suddenly expired. His last words to the princess Isabella were to enjoin upon her not to surrender the territory or the newly conferred crown to anyone but King Richard or the legitimate heir to the throne.

The Count of Champagne who had scarcely reached Acre on his way back to Ascalon, was informed of the murder by a swift messenger, and immediately returned to Tyre. Here an unexpected course of events awaited him.

The funeral of the Marquess Conrad was the first matter requiring attention. It had to be celebrated with all the becoming pomp and magnificence customary at the time. As was usual in the twelfth century the body was opened and the entrails removed and wrapped in a rich silk cloth and placed in a small marble coffer. Then the corpse, having been washed with spiced wine, was enveloped in the skins of stags and placed upon a bier in the great hall of the palace, whilst around it were the lighted candles and censers filling the air with the heavy perfume of burning gums and spices. A crowd of friends of the murdered man stood as mourners within the chamber, and formed groups in the neighbouring apartments and streets, whilst innumerable women with the princess and her attendant ladies, crooned or chanted appropriate dirges.[1]

It was arranged that the Marquess should be buried in the church of the Hospitallers. On the great day of the funeral, at which the Count of Champagne was the chief mourner, an imposing procession escorted the bier covered with a magnificent silk pall from the palace to the hospital. Knights and nobles, with their dames, esquires, sergeants, varlets and men-at-arms, and a vast crowd of the French Crusaders who were still encamped around Tyre awaiting transports to carry them back to Marseilles, made up a funeral cortege which was sufficiently imposing. Within the church of the hospital the Bishop of Beauvais with the abbots and prelates of neighbouring monasteries and cathedrals, celebrated the Mass for the dead with all its impressive ritual, whilst a choir of priests chanted the responses as the herse erected in the centre of the church was asperged with Holy Water amidst clouds of incense and perfume.

At this ceremony the two chief personages present were the widow, the princess Isabella, and Henry, Count of Champagne. Escorted back to their respective palaces, by crowds of enthusiastic adherents, these two found themselves in a rather peculiar position.

Whilst the funeral ceremonies of the Marquess had been taking place, the political atmosphere of Tyre had become overcast with change and a new development. The French who lived in tents outside the city, were disposed to carry matters with a high hand, and made a demand that the territory of Tyre should be handed over to them on behalf of the King of France. To this demand the princess immediately replied that her dying husband had confided his realm to her care to keep until the King of England should visit her, and dispose of it

[1] V. le Duc, "Mobilier, Vie public de la noblesse Féudale," p. 332.

as he thought fit, and therefore she would not surrender it to anyone else.

At this juncture a remarkable thing occurred. The people of Tyre who were largely Italian by race, and had no great love for the French, were enthusiastic in supporting their legitimate princess and the Anglo-Norman interest, immediately set on foot a proposal that Count Henry should marry the princess Isabella and so become *ipso facto* King of the Latin Kingdom. This suggestion was not altogether unwelcome to the Duke of Burgundy and his council, for Count Henry was nephew of both the Kings of England and France.

Events marched with rapidity, and the third day after the funeral of her husband, the much married Isabella was betrothed to the Count of Champagne.[1] At the same time the Count was proclaimed rightful heir to the throne of the Latin Kingdom. At once the news of this election and proposed marriage together with an account of the murder of the Marquess was sent to King Richard at Ascalon, by trusty messengers.

King Richard hearing of the murder, was for a long time silent with astonishment. Then having enquired into the circumstances attending the election of his nephew, he expressed a great satisfaction at the turn which had taken place in the course of affairs. He was aware of the popularity of Count Henry and he foresaw great advantages to all in this arrangement.

Meanwhile the Count, who had declared that he would do nothing in the matter without the assent and advice of his uncle, had become the favoured candidate for the crown on the part of the French at Tyre. At their instigation the princess Isabella was induced to make a formal and public ceremony of visiting the Count in his palace, and presenting him with the keys of the city of Tyre, in acknowledgment of his position as her affianced husband. This was of course an occasion for public jubilation and display : the streets of Tyre were resonant with musical instruments, the housefronts were gay with hangings and carpets spread at every window, and the church bells kept up an intermittent but continual clangour, as Isabella on horseback, surrounded by her feudatories, with the ponderous keys of the city borne before her on a cushion

[1] Cont. Will. Tyre, p. 195.

by the seneschal, paid this visit of ceremony to the prince who was to become her third husband in the course of a few days.[1]

The nuptial ceremony performed on a May morning of 1192 in the cathedral of Tyre by the Archbishop and his suffragans was of the most pompous kind. Surrounded by a numerous court, by the French Crusaders and by the townspeople the ceremony proceeded according to the ritual, but the crowning of the newly wedded pair was for the moment deferred. The young princess, although she had already been twice married could not have been more than twenty-three years old,[2] her husband was a few years her senior. How little the happy pair—for they seem to have had a great affection for each other—could have imagined that within five years time the youthful princess would be called upon to undergo the same ceremony with a fourth husband in the person of Guy de Lusignan's brother the King of Cyprus.

The King of England was soon informed of the marriage ceremony at Tyre, and he acknowledged it, as it is said in the following words to the messengers from the Count: "I congratulate you on the election of Count Henry; and I am very desirous, if it be the will of God, that he should be invested with the government of the kingdom as soon as we have obtained entire possession of the Holy Land. But concerning his marrying the widow of the Marquess, I have no advice to give, for the Marquess seized upon her unlawfully when her husband was alive, and committed adultery by his intercourse with her. Let Count Henry take the kingdom, and the city of Acre, with all its appurtenances, Tyre, and Jaffa, and the whole of the land, if it so please God, for ever. Tell him also in my name, to set out for the campaign as quickly as possible and bring the French with him; for I purpose to take Darum in spite of all the opposition of the Saracens."[3]

The message from King Richard pleased everyone, and the French and Anglo-Normans were equally jubilant and satisfied, for Count Henry being a nephew of both the

---

[1] It. Regis. Angl., V., 35. [2] M. Latrie "Histoire" I., 145.
[3] It. Regis. Angl. V., 34. Darum was a fortress near the seacoast between El Arish and Gaza, now known as Ed-darum, but the ruins of crusading times seem to have disappeared. It was on the principal line of communication between Egypt and Jerusalem in the twelfth century.

AN ENGLISH KING. 149

French and English kings, it was hoped that by this union happier times would be inaugurated, and a return made to peace and concord between the two great western races.

On the completion of his nuptials with the princess Isabella, the Count of Champagne assumed the style and dignity of Seigneur of the Kingdom of Jerusalem but not the title of " King." He however sent the necessary governors to Acre, Jaffa, and other fortresses, and to all his dominions to hold them in his name, and under his lordship. He then published a proclamation calling on all to get ready for the expedition under the King of England against Darum.

At the end of May, Count Henry with his friends the Duke of Burgundy and the French Crusaders began their march down the coast to assist King Richard in the neighbourhood of Ascalon and Gaza. As the army approached Acre, the citizens about 60,000 in number came out along the northern road to meet it with dances and music. This immense number of people crowded round their new lord with every demonstration of joy and satisfaction, whilst the clergy came bearing their reliquaries from every church, and swinging censers which filled the air with the perfume of frankincense. Banners and pennons fluttering in the air, the gay dresses of the women stationed alongside the road, and the glittering steel of hauberks and arms created a brilliant spectacle.

In Acre the Count was led by a procession of ecclesiastics into the cathedral church ; accompanying him was his newly wedded princess, whom he refused to leave behind, as he could not yet endure to be without her. Within the cathedral the princely couple were led to the steps of the altar, where kneeling with great devotion they were permitted to venerate and kiss a fragment of the True Cross, and other holy relics. Then escorted to the royal palace, a banquet was prepared, and everyone strove to do honour to their new lord and lady.

At the time of the Marquess' murder in Tyre the King of England had been much perturbed by the messages coming from the Chancellor and others whom he had left in charge of his European realms. Subsequent news had been even more disquieting and he felt that his return to the west was now imperative. He found it hard to tear himself away from his cherished hopes of recovering the Latin Kingdom, and so for some little time longer he continued his fruitless struggle—but this has little to do with the History of Cyprus.

Master Geoffrey the Cellarer in his diary of events gives us to understand that King Guy of Jerusalem at the moment of the murder of the Marquess of Montferrat was living at Acre to where he had returned with Stephen de Turnham on the 20th December 1191. But it is presumable that he would retire from the city on hearing of the triumphal approach of his successful rival Count Henry from Tyre in the following May, and the only place to retire to would be along the coast towards Ascalon.

On rejoining King Richard at Ascalon, Guy de Lusignan, occupying the strange position of a king from whom all authority had been taken away by usurpers who still professed to recognize his legitimate kingship, was received with all due honour and ceremony. A conference between Guy and Richard was immediately held, at which were discussed the recent events in the island of Cyprus, the dissatisfaction of the Templars with their bargain, and the possibility of rearranging matters in such a way as to allow of the putative King of Jerusalem taking the place of the Military Order, and retiring from a position on the mainland which seemed to be untenable.

Richard favoured the idea of this arrangement by which the dispossessed monarch of the Holy Land could withdraw with dignity leaving the country and its defence in the hands of more active and capable hands. The Chancellor of the Kingdom of Jerusalem, Pierre d'Angouleme, Bishop of Tripoli, warmly seconded the proposal, and what was still more important, brought with him the offers of certain rich merchants living in Tripoli, to advance the 40,000 besants which it was necessary to provide in some way for the repayment to the Templars,[1] but as to this part of the business, King Richard showed himself very complaisant, and exacted no personal security from King Guy; but at the same time retained the pledged fortress belonging to the Templars.

---

[1] Cont. Will. Tyre, 187. M. Latrie "Histoire" I., 37.

AN ENGLISH KING. 151

The loan advanced by the merchants of Tripoli was to be paid in besants d'or, to the credit of the Temple Order within two months from the taking possession of the island. The ownership of the property was therefore at first divided between the Templars and the King of Jerusalem, the King of England continuing to hold the pledge for the payment of the balance of the original sale price of 100,000 besants d'or, for which the Templars were apparently held responsible to King Richard.

King Guy took possession of his new realm at the end of May, 1192,[1] whilst King Richard was still engaged in the last struggles of his campaign in Palestine, a campaign which he vainly hoped would place his nephew the Count of Champagne firmly on a Levantine throne of possibly a more ambitious kind than the former Latin kingdom had ever been. Richard is credited by some of the old chroniclers with a changed attitude towards King Guy, almost amounting to treachery, in the few months which elapsed between May and October 1192, when he finally abandoned the country, vowing to return with a vast army within a year or two with the intention of conquering all that had been lost to the Saracens, and much more, including the whole of the Byzantine Empire.

King Richard also avowed his intention of dispossessing Guy de Lusignan of his new island kingdom, for which he said the King of Jerusalem would never be able to pay,[2] and his mind seemed to be centred entirely on the advancement of his nephew.

Before leaving Palestine, King Richard endeavoured to have an interview with Guy and requested his attendance at Acre. The King of Jerusalem accordingly passed over from Cyprus to visit his suzerain, but when he arrived no King Richard was there. A rumour or suspicion of foul play to be practised on him, caused Guy to secure his escape on board his galley, which putting to sea under pretext of visiting Jaffa in search of King Richard, was soon back again in Cyprus. After this event there began to be evidences of open hostility between the Count of Champagne and the brothers of the house of Lusignan.[3]

[1] M. Latrie "Histoire" p. 50.
[2] Ibid, p. 51. At the time of his death King Richard was proposing to make preparations for another Levantine expedition.
[3] Cont. Will. Tyre, p. 202.

One sees for the first time, during the third Crusade, in the midst of a war characterised by barbarism and religious fanaticism, the most extraordinary evidences of courtesy, and even a friendliness between the chiefs of the contending forces. The amicable relations between Richard I. and Saladin, and even more with the Sultan's brother Sephardin, gave rise to the strangest mediæval legends, and afforded Sir Walter Scott a sufficient theme for one of his most celebrated novels. That such relations between Christian and Moslem princes and chiefs really existed is borne out by the story of the embassy sent by King Guy to Saladin to announce his having acquired the lordship of Cyprus from the King of England. It is also stated that the new Lord of Cyprus presented a request that the famous Sultan would advise him as to the best means by which he would be able to rule and keep his realm in peace and prosperity. To this embassy Saladin is said to have replied, " I never liked King Guy, but since he has addressed this enquiry to me, I must reply as well as I can, for one man consulted by another even if his enemy should respond frankly to such confidence. I will therefore counsel King Guy, that if he wishes to keep the island of Cyprus, he should give his attention entirely to it."[1]

But King Guy de Lusignan was not long to enjoy such peace and contentment as the comparative security of an island realm usually brings to its possessor. In the month of April, 1194, he died, at the early age of about thirty-five, after a putative reign as King of Jerusalem of six years, and an actual lordship of Cyprus of less than two.

In the short space of two years the newly created government of Cyprus, under Guy de Lusignan, could not pretend to establish those institutions of law and order which the country required under the changed conditions of its existence. Cyprus had passed from being a Byzantine province or theme, into an European feudal kingdom, but the change took many years in the process of development. The most potent element in the more complete transformation of the island at this period was the influx of Europeans driven away by the Saracen invasion of the Holy Land and Syria from their settlements of fifty or

[1] M. Latrie, " Histoire," I. 42.

a hundred years before. Without this influx of strangers into the island the lordship of Guy de Lusignan would have had small chance of developing into the future Kingdom of Cyprus and Jerusalem.

On the death of Guy de Lusignan without any legitimate descendant, the Lordship of Cyprus, which at this date was distinct from the Kingdom of Jerusalem, devolved upon his next of kin, his brother Geoffroy. The fraternal inheritance was however rejected by Geoffroy, and his place was taken with the consent of the already constituted Cypriot feudatories, by the third brother of the Lusignan family, Amaury, Count of Jaffa, and Constable of the Latin Kingdom. At this time Count Amaury was living on his domains in the south of Palestine, at serious variance with Count Henry of Champagne, who had endeavoured to eject him from his position as Constable but was unable to do so because he himself had never assumed the title of King of Jerusalem, always dreaming of a return to France. Although the husband of the royal heiress to the crown, he was neither recognized as King presumptive, nor as regent, or bailiff, and his powers were too limited to allow of his dismissing the great officers of the crown such as the Constable, although he had committed the effective functions of the office to a member of the Ibelin family.[1]

[1] M. Latrie, " Histoire," I., 121.

Heraldic badge of the Ibelins of Beyrout. One of the earliest authentic armorial bearings.

CHAPTER XIV.

IMMEDIATELY on his arrival in Cyprus in the summer of 1194, the new Lord of Cyprus, Amaury, found it necessary to introduce various reforms in the government of the country, which had become very corrupt and irregular under the feeble rule of Guy. One of his first acts was to obtain a distinct recognition by the European powers of his feudal position under the title of " King." For this purpose he made application to the Pope and the Emperor, in accordance with the custom of the period.[1]

Richard Cœur de Lion, as King of England, had conquered Cyprus and raised it into the position of a feudal lordship, but there had been no question of making it a separate kingdom, because Richard's policy had been to keep it for a future date, when he hoped to return and found a much more important Latin Kingdom, either under himself or under his nephew the Count of Champagne, of which Cyprus was to have been part. But Richard had been in a German prison for two years, and his protegée was always chafing at being detained in the Levant, so that the prospects of a vast Eastern Empire seemed but a dream—less realizable even than had been the Third Crusade.

As a man of great practical political experience, Count Amaury saw the necessity which existed for this recognition by the Church and the State of feudal Europe, without

[1] Mas Latrie I., 126.

AN ENGLISH KING. 155

which neither the European settlers nor the natives of Cyprus would become his obedient subjects. For the object in view, Renier de Giblet, a descendant of an old Syrian family established in Cyprus, was selected as the envoy, and on the fête of All Saints (1st November 1195) he arrived at the imperial palace of Gelnhausen on the Rhine.

At the moment of the arrival of the embassy from the Lord of Cyprus, the Emperor Henry VI. was making arrangements for the great expedition or crusade of the year 1197. The homage of Amaury as King of Cyprus was accepted, and it was ordered that the sceptre implying his royal dignity should forthwith be sent him by the hands of the Archbishops of Trani, and Brindisi, whilst the crowning ceremony was to be performed by the Emperor himself when he should visit the island in the course of his crusading pilgrimage during the ensuing year.

But all the elaborate arrangements so carefully prepared for this coronation were frustrated by the sudden death of Henry VI. at Messina who, however, before he died, confided the matter to the hands of Conrad, Bishop of Hildersheim, Chancellor of the Empire.[1]

After the death of the Emperor, part of the German fleet which had assembled at Messina at the beginning of September 1197, was directed to sail to Cyprus, having on board the Bishop of Hildersheim and his attendants. The ships arrived at Amathus about the 20th September, and Count Amaury received the bearer of the imperial commission with becoming honour and display.

The bishop having landed amidst the usual ceremonies and attendance of officials at the quay, was escorted by the future king and a great many of his courtiers to Nicosia, as the large village which had been constituted the capital of the island by the first Latin settlers was now called.

The castle at Nicosia, the building of which had been begun by the Templars in 1191, was now in a more complete condition, and was combined with a royal residence. A church of the Latins with a body of clergy attached had been instituted on the site of the present cathedral, and of this earlier building two ancient doorways in the

[1] Cont. Will. Tyre, p. 210.

Provençal style of architecture are still preserved on the north side of the existing edifice. Within this church the coronation was arranged to be celebrated.

At exactly the same date when Amaury's envoy to the Emperor was offering his homage for the crown of Cyprus, an embassy of an ecclesiastical kind was approaching the Pope with the object of establishing a Latin hierarchy in the island. The Pope (Celestine III.) received the proposal with some degree of caution before permitting his name to be used for the purpose. He demanded to know how the bishops and priests were to be supported, and when it was suggested that stipends would be provided, he refused to sanction a system which would interfere with the independence of the clergy. After much deliberation it was at last decided that an adequate endowment in real estate should be provided by the new government, and with this agreement, two papal commissioners were appointed to arrange for an ecclesiastical establishment such as Count Amaury desired. The two commissioners selected were the Archdeacons of Laodicea (Lattakia) and Lydda. The Archdeacon of Laodicea is only mentioned in the papal documents as "Magister B." he became Bishop of Paphos ; the Archdeacon of Lydda was named Alain, and he was appointed to the newly constituted archdiocese of Nicosia, as primate of Cyprus. The last named " being elected by the chapter of Nicosia, during 1196, was consecrated by the Archbishop of Nazareth, assisted by the Bishops of Bethlehem and Acre."[1]

The coronation of the first Latin King of Cyprus, was a great event in its history. By this act the island was declared to be an integral part of the European confederation of states under the ægis of the Holy Roman Empire. With an account of the ceremony on this important occasion the story of the Third Crusade and the conquest of Cyprus may be fittingly concluded.

On the day before the coronation, a great throne raised on several steps had been arranged at one side of the small church which served as the cathedral of the new capital of Nicosia, and the building had been placed in the guardianship of the sergeants of the royal bodyguard.

---

[1] Hackett, "Church of Cyprus," pp. 537, 564.

AN ENGLISH KING. 157

This was on a Saturday, as a coronation, always took place on a Sunday. During the night preceding the day of the great ceremony, the king-elect entered the church, and kneeling amidst the shadowy forms of saints and angels depicted on the chancel screen, devoutly passed a short time in prayer.

The great village of Nicosia was all astir with a vast crowd of peasantry attracted by the prospect of viewing a grand display of pageantry by their new Latin lords, on that brilliant morning of seven hundred years ago— a morning at the time of year when the first showers of rain after the summer drought are giving a foretaste of the beautiful vernal "garden season" of the Levant. The gaily embroidered dresses of the villagers enlivened the scene, and here and there the sombre figure of a village priest clad in black and purple, with his singular tubular hat suggestive of a strange antiquity, gave a curious note of contrast.

With the first bells of Prime (6.0 a.m.) the king-elect, surrounded by the nobles and feudatories, the knights and men-at-arms, and all the adherents to the new constitution about to be inaugurated in Cyprus, was conducted, amidst the flourishing of horns and trumpets, and the beating of drums, to the cathedral. In the procession were the new Archbishop of Nicosia, the new Bishop of Paphos, preceding the Imperial Chancellor, the Bishop of Hildersheim; Adolphus Count of Holstein, as a great noble of the Empire, represented the Emperor in a lay capacity. The noble families of the Latin Kingdom who had already in the first years of the occupation transferred themselves to Cyprus, were represented by such names as Nefin, Aleman, Dampierre, Blanchegarde, Nores, De Bries, Mimars, and a host of others whose memory still survives in place-names or on tombstone fragments in different parts of the island.

At the door of the church, the dignitaries in the procession were solemnly sprinkled with Holy Water amid clouds of incense, and then conducted to their seats within the chancel screen and on either side of the altar. Meanwhile the Holy Chrism for anointment, the crown studded with jewels, the two sceptres, the sword and golden spurs, and a mantle, a dalmatic, and a pair of shoes, all of blue silk embroidered with gold fleurs-de-lys, had been deposited upon the altar.[1]

The Bishop of Hildersheim now prepared to consecrate the new king before celebrating Mass ; turning to Amaury he said : " Sire, we require you to concede to us and to the churches committed to our rule, our canonical privileges, and due law and justice, and the same protection as that which the king himself enjoys within his own kingdom." To this the king elect replied by giving his assent and promises.

Te Deum was next chanted by the cantors and the choir, during which the Bishop of Hildersheim and the Archbishop taking Amaury by the hands conducted him to the steps of the altar, where he prostrated himself and so remained until the conclusion of the *Te Deum*.

The next act in the ceremonial was for the king-elect to divest himself of his ordinary attire, until he stood before the altar in nothing more than a pair of drawers, a shirt, and an undershirt of silk. The shirts were open low down back and front, and confined with silver pins.

The Chamberlain of the kingdom then approached the king, who was seated on a faldstool before the altar, and put on his feet the shoes which he had taken from the altar. At the same time another high official brought the golden spurs and fitted them to the shoes, but immediately removed them.

The bishop carrying the sword in its scabbard descended the altar steps, and caused it to be ceremoniously girded on the king, and then removed. Then he drew it from its scabbard, and presented the naked blade to the king with the words : " Take the sword given you with the blessing of God," meanwhile the choir chanted an anthem and the king having made an offering of the sword at the altar, it was placed in the hands of the Constable of the kingdom, Baldwin de Bethshan, whose duty it was to carry it before the king during the remainder of the ceremony and on the return to the palace.

[1] Authorities for the greater part of this description of a royal coronation in the twelfth century, are Viollet le Duc " Mobilier," p. 305, *et seq.* who gives the text of a description of the coronation of Louis VII., in 1179, as registered in the Chambre des Comptes of Paris. This was no doubt the model for all such ceremonies in the Frank Kingdoms of the Levant at the same period.

AN ENGLISH KING. 159

The bishop, taking a paten into his hands, and saying the prayer of consecration, proceeded to prepare the Holy Chrism for the ceremony of anointing : he then seated himself on a faldstool in front of the altar, and the king knelt in front of him.

The king's shirts were unfastened, and the bishop with a morsel of wool dipped in the chrism, anointed him on some parts of his body : the top of his head, the breast, between the shoulders, and on each shoulder and armpit ; the Holy Oil being carefully removed with a linen cloth by an acolyte and ceremonially burnt in a brazier within the church. At each of these acts of anointment, the bishop repeated the words : " I anoint thee with the Holy Oil in the name of the Trinity." The bishops present repeated the prayers and words of consecration whilst the choir chanted anthems.

The ceremony of anointment being concluded, the Chamberlain of the kingdom proceeded to clothe the king, as he now had become, in the royal robes which had been deposited on the altar : first the dalmatic or sleeved tunic, then the royal mantle. The bishop then placed a great finger-ring on the middle finger of the king's right hand, with the words : " Take this ring, symbol of the Holy Faith." After reciting a prayer, the sceptre was brought from the altar and the bishop placed it in the king's right hand, saying : " Take the sceptre, symbol of the royal power." Then after a prayer a second sceptre, called the " Rod of Justice," was brought, and the bishop placed this in the king's left hand, with the words : " Take the rod of power to administer Justice and Equity."

Vested in the royal clothing and ornaments Amaury de Lusignan having become the duly anointed King of Cyprus, the ceremony of his coronation followed. The Chancellor, or highest dignitary next to the King, then summoned the principal barons by name and order, to stand at the sides of the King, whilst the Bishop taking the jewelled crown from the altar placed it on the King's head, all those who were nearest assisting to support it with their hands ; the Bishop saying : " God crown thee with the crown of glory and justice." Then after a prayer he addressed the King saying : " Be firm, and hold the realm to which you have succeeded as heir to your brother." The ceremonial was brought to a conclusion by a recital of the homage which the King had undertaken to perform towards the Emperor, with certain prayers and anthems.

The King having now been anointed and crowned, was led by bishops and barons in a solemn procession from the sanctuary to the throne on steps at the side of the church. Here he seated himself, whilst the Constable stood by holding the naked sword, and the greater barons and officers of the kingdom seated themselves on the surrounding steps. In this way the King was visible to all, and the " recognition by the people " took place, the seneschal advanced and proclaimed in a loud voice the titles of the new king, commanding the acquiescence of the assembled nobles and feudatories. The " vivats " of the people were led by the choir of priests surrounding the altar, and if somewhat lacking in response by the crowd of natives outside the church, their place was supplied by the sounds of martial music, trumpets, and nacaires.

The Mass was now celebrated : at the reading of the gospel the King stood up, and the crown was removed from his head, whilst the Archbishop of Nicosia taking the book from the deacon, carried it to the King in order that he might kiss it. At the offertory, a loaf of bread, a silver vase of wine, and twelve pieces of gold were presented as the King's offering.

During the canon of the Mass, after the Pax Domini, the Bishop of Hildersheim, the Archbishop and other prelates present approached the King on his throne, and each gave him the customary kiss on the cheek.

At the communion the King was again led processionally up to the altar by the great officers of State to receive the consecrated wafer ; after which the bishop removed the jewelled crown from the King's head and substituted a circlet of gold fleur-de-lisé. Mass having been concluded with the customary " Ite missa est," the King was divested of his inner silk shirt by stripping it off beneath the royal robes, and it was ceremonially burnt in the brazier at the side of the sanctuary.

Once more the trumpets and drums pealed forth their notes, the people shouted, the royal procession issued from the portals of the small cathedral which had been built by the Latins on the site of the present cathedral of Santa Sofia, and the first Latin King of Cyprus, Amaury, was escorted back to the newly built palace of Nicosia.

AN ENGLISH KING. 161

CYPRVS Z IERUSALEM
Arms of Amaury after his marriage with Isabella Queen of Jerusalem.

ADDENDA.

PAGE 6.

THE arms and accoutrement of the twelfth century soldier need more particular reference. During the earlier Crusades plate armour was unknown, the warrior depending entirely on his hauberk or sleeved coat of chain-mail which reached from his neck to his knees, with leggings or stockings also of chain-mail. The head was also protected with a kind of hood of mail which was sometimes attached to, or formed part of the hauberk when the " pot " helmet or cap was not used. A steel cap with a bar descending over the nose, to protect the face, was also provided with a chain-mail covering to the neck and sides of the face. Towards the end of the century the larger " pot " helmet, with holes and slits in it for seeing and breathing, was used as a head covering by the knights, but the movable visor did not appear until the introduction of plate armour in the fourteenth century.

Amongst the best illustrations of the twelfth century chain-mail armour remaining are the effigies of the two Williams Longsword on their tombs in Salisbury Cathedral, the elder of whom was son of Henry II. and Rosamund Clifford, which represent this type of armour without a helmet, and the great seal of Edward I. who is pourtrayed thereon as wearing chain-mail with a " pot " helmet of an ornamental kind, surmounted by a royal crown, so late as 1272.[1]

The chain-mail hauberk was always covered by a surcoat of linen or silk, on which were appropriately embroidered the heraldic badges of the knights, after the introduction of such distinguishing marks in the course of the Third Crusade.

" Heater " or " kite " shaped shields are perhaps the most characteristic features of the armour of the twelfth century knight. They were usually made of elm wood, covered with leather and appropriately painted. The use of the shield was not confined to the purpose implied by its name, but in the art of self defence it was handled in sword play, in the same manner as the dagger was part of the rapier fencing equipment at a later period.

Chain-mail armour work over leather jerkins, and in some cases, supplemented by leather hardened in a particular way : boiling in oil, and hammering on an anvil ; was probably not so impervious to lethal weapons as the plate armour of a subsequent age. It was worn by the Crusaders, and also in a very similar manner by their Saracen foes as the only possible kind of iron protection to the human body in battle, endurable in a hot climate. As such it remained in use amongst eastern nations until modern times.

The weapons of the Crusaders were : for the knights on horseback, a somewhat light form of lance, used for charging or hurling at the enemy, and a double edged sword strapped on the left hip by a waist belt. On his right saddle-bow the horseman usually carried a mace or battle-axe.

The infantry, or men-at-arms were provided with heavy lances or pikes, and " bills " of different forms. They also carried battle-axes, maces, and swords.

The famous English longbows used at Crécy and Poitiers with so much effect, in the fourteenth century, were of little importance in the time of Richard Cœur de Lion, but the crossbow was perhaps the most important weapon of his period. Richard was himself an adept in

[1] Kingsford's " Crusades "

its use, and his death by a well aimed quarrel from the walls of the chateau de Chaluz possibly shows that chain mail was hardly proof against what Anna Comnena calls " the diabolical device " of the arbalest.

The mode of fighting and the equipment of the Crusaders were to a very great extent influenced by the contemporary customs of their Saracen enemies, and many developments of the mediæval art of war are traceable to an eastern source.

Military discipline and drill as we understand such things at the present day could have been but little practised in the mediæval armies. Hand to hand combat was the method of fighting at that period, and only on certain occasions were the men-at-arms required to form into square or line, in the simple manœuvre of lowering their pikes with a holdfast in the ground, and thus to form a serried rank to receive a cavalry charge—a rare event in Europe where the cavalry consisted of isolated knights on their chargers surrounded by their feudal levies.

Every form of exercise with arms of all kinds to be used in single combat was of course sedulously cultivated, as well as shooting at a target with bow and crossbow. Every man, whether knight on horseback, or man-at-arms on foot had a more independent position in the mélée than would be possible in the course of a modern battle. Those were the days when every man was expected to study the art of self defence—whether in the great battles of an international kind or in the daily strife of more domestic interests, and to be ready with such arms as he was accustomed to.

As the knights of a great mediæval army, clad in close fitting chain-mail from head to foot, carrying the characteristic " flat-iron " shaped shield on their left arms, whilst the right hand grasped sword, or axe, or mace of varied forms, and astride of their war-horses, entered the field of battle, each of them formed the centre of a " clump of spears," and was surrounded by his men-at-arms with their pikes, javelins, and billhooks. Each knight, to some extent in the position of a modern " officer," became a tower of strength to his men, directing, controlling, encouraging them as the case might be : when he fell in the mélée, his men were dispersed, or joined the standard of some other feudal lord. The forefront of a battle line in the twelfth century consisted of these "clumps of spears" with the knight and his squires a central figure of each group. Behind them stood the bowmen launching flights of arrows at the enemy; still more in the rear were the marshals with their attendant trumpeters whose duty was to convey the general instructions from the sovereign prince or king who usually commanded in chief, and whose banner borne before him constituted the rallying point of the whole army. At the moment of the mêlée, the air was filled with the battle-cries of the feudal retainers, and the trumpeters sounded the point of war "corps à corps."

A mediæval camp was a brilliant spectacle : the glare of bright colour, the sparkle of a thousand points in burnished arms and armour exhilarated the soldiers, and interested the spectators. The pomp and circumstance of war rendered the profession of arms attractive in a way which has disappeared along with its gaudy trappings, and its life of display. But certain features of a mediæval camp would appear shocking to our modern and refined sensibilities. The gambling, drunkenness, and profligacy, the terrible social degradation and all the evils attendant on the growth of a vast military class, could not be concealed beneath the splendours of mediæval pageantry. High in the air amongst the tent groups were reared gibbets, gaunt frames of wood on which hung a few dead bodies tainting the evening breeze, and causing a shiver to those unaccustomed to the sight, or whose attention had been attracted by the croaking of attendant kites and crows. In those days the gibbet formed perhaps a very necessary accompaniment to the administration of justice in a military camp.

PAGE 8.

Richard Hakluyt, in his "Navigations" published in 1599 gives a list of ancient writers of travels, and amongst them mentions the author of the "Itinerarium Regis Anglorum" as an Observant Friar and a Canon of the church of the Trinity, London, which stood in the place now called the Minories. But this statement is evidently incorrect because there were no Minorites or Observant

AN ENGLISH KING.

Friars in existence before the confirmation of the Franciscan Order in 1223, their first appearance in England is said to have been in 1226. The narrative of Geoffrey de Vinsauf unfortunately breaks off in 1194, with the return of King Richard from his German captivity, but there is nothing to indicate whether he wrote it in England or in Palestine. It may therefore be assumed that he was a Benedictine, an idea which his learned pedantry and classical quotations seem to support.

PAGE 37.

Richard of Devizes, a Carthusian monk of Witham in Essex, who wrote a chronicle of Richard I.'s reign, gives a curious and interesting account of the episode of Messina besieged by the Anglo-Normans. The "Griffons," before King Richard's arrival in Sicily were more powerful than all the mighty of that region, and having moreover always hated the people beyond the Alps, and now irritated by recent occurrences were more inveterate than ever, kept the peace with all who claimed the King of France for their master, but sought to wreak the vengeance of their wrongs on the King of England and his tailed followers, for the Greeks and Sicilians followed the king about and called them "tailed English." The origin of this insulting joke, or piece of chaff, is very obscure; at one time the inhabitants of Wales and Cornwall were credited with caudal appendages, by presumably their Anglo-Norman neighbours; it is curious to find the same idea prevalent in the extreme south of Europe applied to the Anglo-Normans themselves. "All intercourse with the country is denied the English by proclamation; they are murdered both day and night by forties and fifties, whenever they are found unarmed...... The King of England, enraged by these disorders, like the fiercest lion, vented his anger in a manner worthy that noble beast. His fury astounded his nearest friends and his whole court, the famous princes of his army sat around his throne each according to his rank, and if anyone dared to raise his eyes to look him in the face, it was very easy to read in the ruler's countenance what he silently considered in his mind. After a long and deep silence, the King disburdened his indignant lips as follows :

"O, my soldiers! my kingdom's strength and crown! who have endured with me a thousand perils,........ do you now see how a cowardly rabble insults us? shall we vanquish Turks and Arabs? shall we be a terror to nations, the most invincible?........when we have turned our backs before vile and effeminate Griffons?........ let everyone follow what he may have chosen, but I will either die here, or will revenge these wrongs common to me and you. If hence I depart alive, Saladin will see me only a conqueror; will you depart and leave me, your king, alone to meet the conflict?

"The king had scarcely well concluded his harangue, when all his brave and valiant men burst out troubled only that their lord appeared to mistrust them........ As the clamour, hushed by the rulers gravity, subsided, 'I am pleased,' said he 'with what I hear; you refresh my spirit by your readiness to cast off your disgrace...... Messina shall be taken by me in the first place, the Griffons shall either ransom themselves or be sold. If King Tancred do not speedily satisfy me for my sister's dowry and the legacy of King William, which falls to me in right of my father, after the depopulation of his kingdom, he shall be compelled to restore them fourfold........ Let two thousand knights (whose hearts are not in their boots!) and a thousand archers, be made ready within two days. Let the law be enforced without remission; the footsoldier who flies shall lose one foot, the knight be deprived of his girdle. Let every man, according to military discipline, be disposed in exact array, and on the third day, at the sound of the horn, let them follow me.' The assembly separated with the greatest applause; the King having relaxed the sternness of his countenance, was seen returning thanks for their goodwill with his wonted affability of expression.

"It wonderfully fell out that not even the King's enemies could pretend that his cause was unjust. On the third day when the army was to be led forth to battle, very early in the morning, Richard, Archbishop of Messina, the Archbishops of Monreale, Pisa, Rouen and Auch, the Bishops of Evreux, Bayonne, and Carnot, Philip, King of the French, the Duke of Burgundy, the Counts of Nevers and Perch, and many followers of the King of France, and all who were supposed to have any influence

AN ENGLISH KING. 167

with the English, came reverently to the King of England, that they might cause satisfaction for all his complaints to be given to his content. The King after long and earnest solicitation, is prevailed on by the entreaty of such honourable men, and commits the matter to be settled by their arbitration.

"The King's army stood in readiness with solemn silence awaiting the herald, from the rising of the sun, and the peace proposals had protracted the day until the third hour, when unexpectedly a voice proclaimed very distinctly before the gates, ' To arms, to arms, men ! Hugo Bruno is taken and being murdered by the Griffons, all he has is being plundered, and his men are being slaughtered.' This cry of the breach of peace confounded those who were treating for the peace, and the King of France exclaimed, ' I take it that God has hated these men, and hardened their hearts that they may fall into the hand of the destroyer.' Then running to the English King's tent he found him girding on his sword, whom he thus addressed : ' I am witness before all men, whatever be the consequence, that thou art blameless, if at length thou takest arms against the cursed Griffons.' When he had said this he withdrew into the city.

" The King of England proceeds in arms ; the terrible standard of the dragon is borne in front unfurled (perhaps the lion-banner is meant ?) while behind the King the sound of the trumpet excites the army. The sun shone brightly on the golden shields, and the mountains were resplendent in their glare. They marched cautiously and in order, and the matter was managed without show. The Griffons having closed the city gates, stood armed at the battlements of the walls and towers, as yet fearing nothing, and incessantly discharged darts upon their enemy. The King acquainted with nothing better than the taking of cities by storm, let their quivers be emptied first, and then at length made his first assault by his archers who preceded the army. The sky is hidden under a shower of arrows, a thousand darts pierce the shields appearing on the ramparts, nothing could save the rebels from the force of the darts. The walls are abandoned by their guards, because no one could look out of doors, without receiving an arrow in his eye before he could shut it."

The King captured the city with but little resistence, and took every hold within it, even to Tancred's palace and the lodgings of the French King and the quarters around, which he spared in respect of the King who was his feudal lord. (The King of England owed fealty to the French crown for certain of his continental possessions). His standards were planted on the towers, through the whole circuit of the city, and having withdrawn his army, and his hostages which he had taken from the city and the surrounding country, he returned victorious to his camp.

PAGE 49.

The government of England had been committed to the care of William Longchamp Bishop-elect of Ely, during the absence of Richard Cœur de Lion on the Crusade. The King left England after his coronation for Normandy and his continental dominions on December 12, 1189. William the Bishop-elect, who was consecrated on December 31, 1189, by Baldwin, Archbishop of Canterbury, had already been constituted the Chancellor of the kingdom, an honour partly due to his paying three thousand pounds of silver for it and partly to the new King's favour. He is described as of a goodly person, making up in mind for the shortness of his stature, but as a tyrant, and more cruel than a wild beast to all those his enemies. In that strange and most anomalous European world during the middle ages, the types of humanity which governed it were of the most diverse characters, actuated by motives which it is very difficult to appreciate at the present day. The reasons which can have induced Richard Cœur de Lion to select such a man as the Bishop of Ely as his confidant in place of Ralph de Glanville, his former steward and chancellor when Count of Poitou, whom he turned off in an ignominious manner after years of faithful service, can only be attributed to one of those political intrigues which marked the course of his reign. Before his departure from Messina, Richard commissioned Walter Archbishop of Rouen to carry letters to the chancellor, on his return to his diocese, with a recommendation that the Archbishop's counsel and advice should be used in affairs of the regency. He also committed his mother, Queen Eleanor, to the Archbishop's care, and after due ceremonial leave takings and affectionate embraces the Queen and the Archbishop set out on their return journey through Italy and central France towards London. But by the time of their arrival in Normandy the revolutions and divisions amongst the different classes and races constituting the realm of the Anglo-Norman Kings were already breaking forth with all the greater force, consequent upon the absence of the legitimate sovereign, and the machinations of his perfidious brother John. The history of England at this period of turmoil and confusion, is a vast subject to which only a bare reference can be made in this connexion.

PAGE 67.

De Mas Latrie begins his " Histoire de l'ile de Chypre " with the advent on its shores of the Crusaders led by Richard I., King of England. At the foot of each page devoted to this portion of the subject is a copious list of authorities : Vinsauf, William of Newbury, Roger of Howden, Benedict of Peterboro', Coggeshale, etc., but especially the anonymous continuator of the " History " by William of Tyre.

It would appear that Mas Latrie must have relied chiefly on the " Cont. de Guill. de Tyr " for his particulars of the Anglo-Norman occupation of Cyprus, in preference to the English contemporary authorities, as there seem several definite differences between his modernised version of the landing of the Anglo-Normans in the island and the statements by Vinsauf and Benedict of Peterboro'.

For instance : Mas Latrie states that on the arrival of Richard in the bay of Limassol (meaning Amathus, as the modern Limassol did not then exist) he begged for a supply of drinking water and provisions for his fleet, and that the refusal of this request was the ostensible reason for the subsequent raid. The Crusaders disembarked from their ships at some distance from the town (*i.e.* Amathus) and were astonished to be met by a deputation of Latin residents with the information that the Despot Isaac and his troops had fled, frightened at the prospect of the threatened invasion. That the Crusaders then took possession of the town. (Cont. Guill. de Tyr., p. 164.)

The above account, written in 1261 according to Mas Latrie's own " chronologie " is very unlike the narrative by Geoffrey Vinsauf who seems to have written as an eyewitness at the end of the year 1192.

Benedict of Peterboro' was certainly a contemporary of Richard I., as he had been Court historian to his father Henry II. His account agrees with that of Vinsauf: "they came to land with a rush. The arrows fell like rain upon the grass."

Mas Latrie evidently commits other errors in this part of his "Histoire," such as the description of places which only existed at a much later period—Nicosia, Famagusta, Limassol, and the castles of Hilarion, Buffavento, Cantara, etc.,—as if they were already of importance. Most of these places are not mentioned by Benedict of Peterboro. Records of so remote a period as the twelfth century are preserved in manuscript copies, which are often "improved upon" by later scribes adding geographical references of their own invention to render themselves more intelligible to their contemporaries.

PAGE 87.

Benedict of Peterboro—a chronicler, whose work evidently was written before his death in 1193—mentions that the Armenian prince Leo, *i.e.* Leo II., or the Great, King of Armenia (in 1189, died 1219), visited Cyprus in the company of Guy de Lusignan in 1191.

The Kingdom of Little Armenia, or Cilicia, was an independent sovereignty founded at about the time of the first Crusade (1099) by an Armenian chieftain who is known to history as Rhupen II. or Reuben of the Mountain, meaning Mount Taurus. The success of his enterprise was probably due to the contemporary foundation of the great and powerful principalities of Edessa and Antioch on his eastern frontiers, and his position was immensely strengthened by his alliance with the Latin settlers in northern Syria. The son of Rhupen I., named Constantine, accompanied the Crusaders to Jerusalem and, according to a legend, was created a Marquis by King Godfrey.

Constantine I. of Armenia Minor, was succeeded by about six descendants, the seventh being the Leo II. (or I. according to some accounts) called the "Great," who identified himself completely with the Latin interests

AN ENGLISH KING. 171

in the Levant, and obtained a recognition as a feudatory of the Holy Roman Empire. He was crowned as a Latin king by Conrad, Bishop of Hildersheim, acting as Legate of the Emperor Henry VI. in 1198. This coronation is said to have taken place at Sis, then the capital of the kingdom, in conjunction with the crowning of Amaury II.

With Leo the Great ends the original dynasty of the Rhupenians, his daughter Isabella was married to Philip, the Poitivin Prince of Antioch, who was murdered in 1226. This crime was of course the outcome of a fanatical opposition on the part of many of the Armenians to the Europeanizing efforts of Leo and his crusading friends. Isabella, the widowed heiress of the Rhupenians, was promptly married to a chieftain of the opposition party named Hayton, who reigned until 1270. The crown of Armenia Minor was considered to descend through a succession of grandchildren of Hayton, ending once more in an heiress named Isabella, who again was married to a Latin prince, Amaury de Lusignan, the famous usurper of the Kingdom of Cyprus during the reign of Henry II., the descendants of this marriage coming to an end in 1393 in the person of Leo VI., who, after an adventurous life, was forced to abandon his kingdom and take refuge, first in Spain, afterwards at Paris, where he died in his palace " des Tournelles," and was eventually buried in the royal Abbey of St. Denis.

On the death of Leo VI., the crown of Armenia Minor, now a mere empty title, was assumed by the kings of Cyprus, beginning with James I. de Lusignan, King of Jerusalem, Cyprus, and Armenia, through the descendants of whom the succession seems still to linger in the famous house of the princes of Savoy, and the modern kings of Italy.

In reference to the above outline of the " Latinized " kingdom of " Little Armenia " or Cilicia, it should be noted that whatever the relations between Leo the Great and the Roman Catholic Church may have been in 1198, they seem to have been distinct from what is known as the " Uniat " movement of the Armenian colonies in Poland, Austria, and elsewhere in 1439, recognizing the Pope's supremacy, and conforming to some extent to the Roman Catholic Church. Three centuries later the " Uniats " were chiefly represented and known to Europe by the " Mechitaristi " monks of the convent of St. Lazzaro at Venice, there established by Pope Clement XI., and the Venetian Republic in 1717, after their expulsion from Constantinople by the Gregorian Armenian Patriarch. The Armenian Uniats seem to have been sufficiently numerous in Austria at this period to establish an important university, frequented by students from all parts of Europe.

According to J. de Morgan's "Histoire du peuple Armenien," 1919, Leo the Great should be regarded as Leo I., the first King of the Latinized or New Armenia. He married Sibylla, daughter of Amaury II., King of Jerusalem and Cyprus, and Isabella Plantagenet, great grand-daughter of Fulk V. of Anjou, King of Jerusalem. Thus a Plantagenet Norman strain seems to have penetrated the curious Kingdom of Armenia.

PAGE 103.

One of the most serious errors of detail committed by Mas Latrie is certainly the statement that Berengaria was crowned by the Archbishop of York at Limassol (Amathus). "Histoire" I., 9. The Archbishop of York at the time of the Third Crusade, was Geoffrey, one of the numerous illegitimate children of Henry II., and therefore the King's natural brother. As a partizan of "Earl John," the future King John of England, he was instrumental in the downfall of the Chancellor, William de Longchamp, and at the time of the marriage of Richard and Berengaria in Cyprus was busily engaged in treasonable plots and conspiracies against his legitimate brother and King of England (*vide* Chron. of Richard of Devizes, section 44.)

In making the above criticisms of M.L. de Mas Latrie's learned and admirable "Histoire de l'ile de Chypre,'" there is no intention of detracting from the immense value of this monumental work. Such a work represents the enthusiastic studies of a lifetime patronized by a most liberal government, and will ever remain a monument of erudition to the credit of the author and his patrons in the year 1861.

PAGE 128.

The daughter of Isaac Comnenus had perhaps the most romantic experiences afterwards that could befall any mediæval princess either in history or fiction. At the outset of her life, she was attached to the suite of the new queen of England, Berengaria, travelled with her in Palestine during the crusading campaign, and with her and the dowager queen of Sicily returned to Europe in 1192, escorted by the English baron Stephen de Turnham, the favourite steward of his household to Richard I. According to one story the three ladies journeyed by way of Italy, and at Rome met with the dowager queen of England, Eleanor of Acquitaine. The three queens and this young Cypriot princess then continued their travels, after a stay of six months in the Eternal City, by way of Genoa to Marseilles, where they were received and escorted by the Count of Provence, Alphonso (afterwards King of Arragon) to the confines of Toulouse, where Raymond de St. Gilles, eldest son of Raymond V., Count of Toulouse, awaited them as their guardian, to the Anglo-Norman territories. This gay young cavalier and knight of high degree is said to have accompanied the four ladies as far as the city of Poitiers, and in spite of having been twice married and with a family of several children, he became the successful suitor of Joan, the widowed queen of Sicily, and sister of King Richard. He married this lady in 1196, she died in the same year.

In 1192 the Levantine princess was presumably about fifteen years old. On arriving at Poitiers she was consigned to the guardianship of a noble English family, together with a princess of Brittany, as a campanion, the two girls being in reality very much in the position of state prisoners, and the place of their residence was the castle of Chinon in Touraine. For several years they pursued the course of life which was in those days the fate of the demoiselle of rank and lineage. Household economies, embroidery, spinning and weaving, consumed the days within the vaulted chambers and courtyards of a feudal castle, and the pleasures of the chase on horseback, the rearing of falcons, and the listening to troubadours or wandering musicians afforded a sufficiency of outdoor recreation and exercise.

In the long winter evenings seated by the huge fireplace of the vaulted hall the young Levantine could tell many tales of the mysterious island in the eastern sea where her father had once ruled as "emperor" and despot. She remained at the royal chateau of Chinon, the beloved home of the Plantagenets, for about seven years.

Whilst the young Greek princess, nominally a ward, but in reality a captive in Normandy, was passing into womanhood, and her father was languishing in his prison at Margat, their conqueror the King of England was also a prisoner in the hands of the German Emperor. The Emperor Henry VI., in his tortuous policy and his brigandish actions, was keenly alive to the advantages of keeping Cœur de Lion in his power, with a view to controlling the fate of England and western France. At the same time he wished to profit by the acquisition of Cyprus as a feudal state to be added to the dominions of the Latins or Franks in the Levant : he was in fact initiating that policy which his very remarkable son, the Emperor Frederick II., carried out at a later period, of quarrelling with the Pope and seizing the Latin Kingdom of Jerusalem.

The Emperor Henry VI. had noted the possibilities of becoming the patron of the fallen Despot, Isaac Comnenus, in opposition to the action of King Richard and his protegée Guy de Lusignan, and with this object in view he stipulated that in addition to the enormous ransom to be paid by the English King on regaining his liberty, the ex-Despot and his daughter should be surrendered into his hands. Richard promised much more than he was ever able to perform, and the death of the ex-Despot put an end to that particular line of the emperor's intrigues.

Whilst the fate of Isaac Comnenus hung in the balance, his daughter was regarded as an eligible *parti* by no less a personage than the reigning Count of Toulouse—the brilliant Raymond de St. Gilles who had been her escort when she arrived in France about seven or eight years before. She was now about twenty-three years old, and consequently her natural attractions were added to her ambiguous political value in the eyes of the uxorious Raymond.

The year 1199 was a date of much political change in Europe. In April died Richard Cœur de Lion, and his former foe, Isaac Comnenus, also disappears from history about the same time. The King of France was busy repudiating one wife and marrying another in the manner which seems to have been fashionable at the period, and even within the same year he had remarried the first wife and repudiated the second at the bidding of Pope Innocent III. The emperor was pursuing a new policy in creating kingdoms out of duchies and counties, beginning with that of Bohemia.

The misfortunes of the Despot's daughter now began to accumulate. The much married Raymond de St. Gilles, although recognizing her as his legitimate wife was able to repudiate her in a fashion easy and common enough in the middle ages. This marriage, the result of a mere momentary passion and caprice, endured for merely a few months, and the Levantine princess who seems not to have had children by this her first husband, was succeeded as Countess of Toulouse by a daughter of the King of Arragon. For some time after this event the repudiated Greek wife lived at Marseilles in obscurity and comparative indigence. In the year 1204 a numerous fleet of Flemish ships was filling the old port of Marseilles, carrying pilgrims, warriors, and stores, for the purpose of the fourth Crusade. Once more as in the days of the third Crusade of fifteen years before, the citizens of Marseilles were treated to a spectacle of military display, and to a prospect of very profitable business in the Levant.

This contingent to the Crusade, under the control of Jean de Nesle, Governor of the city of Bruges, was compelled to pass the winter months at Marseilles, awaiting the fine weather when galleys and rowboats could venture over sea. On board this fleet were several German and Burgundian knights, one of whom, a native of the Rhineland, happening to meet the young princess, and hearing her story, formed plans which could only have occurred to an ill-disciplined mind influenced by the wildest romances of a credulous age. He succeeded in marrying the unfortunate Maria, the discarded Countess of Toulouse, and with her sailed for Cyprus, where he had the temerity to land and approach the new king of the island, Amaury, brother of the recently deceased Guy de Lusignan. Having obtained an audience of the newly crowned king, he had the effrontery to claim the lordship of Cyprus in right of his wife the Comnenian princess. " But when the King Amaury heard his request," says the chronicler " he took him for a fool and a vagabond, and commanded him to clear out of the country at once, if he wished to escape with his life." As no one advised him to remain ; he thought it best, under the circumstances, to take this advice, and accordingly retired into Armenia, where he and his unfortunate wife disappeared from history.[1]

It should be mentioned that this apparently preposterous claim to the crown of Cyprus was not made without a certain vague idea of support on the part of the German Emperor who acknowledged the relationship of the Despot's daughter to himself through her mother, the sister of William II. King of Sicily and niece of his wife the Empress Constance. The Despot was in fact a nephew, by marriage, to the Emperor, and on this account the young Fleming who had married his daughter, the ex-Countess of Toulouse, at Marseilles, and who was himself a near relative of Baldwin, Count of Flanders, received a promise of support from his companions who were sailing with him in the crusading fleet. This story is however very unaccountable when we consider that the Emperor had but recently recognised the Lusignan dynasty with the fullest pomp and ceremonial, and at about the same time had also become the suzerain of the Latinized Kingdom of Armenia.

THE CENOTAPHS OF RICHARD I. AND BERENGARIA.

Berengaria of Navarre, Queen of England, Duchess of Normandy and Acquitaine, Countess of Poitou, etc., etc., is commemorated by an interesting cenotaph which has been re-erected to her memory in the north transept of Le Mans Cathedral.

About five miles to the north-east of the beautiful old city of Le Mans are the scanty ruins of the Abbey of Epau ; here in the days of the royalist enthusiasm after the great revolution, this monument was discovered, and on the 2nd December, 1821, it was solemnly removed into the Cathedral to refill one of the empty spaces caused by the revolutionary vandalism of nearly thirty years before.

Berengaria was born about 1160, being the eldest daughter of Sancho VI., King of the somewhat elusive realm of Navarre, which at different periods has extended on both

[1] Schlumberger " Principautes Franques du Levant " 1877, p. 47. Mas Latrie, " Histoire " I. 158.

AN ENGLISH KING. 177

sides of the Pyrenees, but is now only recognised as a province of Spain. After her marriage to Richard I. in Cyprus, and adventures in the Holy Land, she returned to Sicily, and we next hear of her residing at Chinon, where King John visited her and satisfied her demands for a dowry, in the year 1201. This dowry was in the form of an annual income, but in 1220 she seems to have accepted a sum of money as composition. She also seems to have resigned her titles of Duchess of Acquitaine and Poitou to the old queen Eleanor who retained these possessions until her death in 1204.

About the year 1230, Berengaria built, or rebuilt, the abbey of Epau, amongst the sandy heaths of Maine. She presumably lived near by, perhaps in Le Mans, for there seems to have been a tradition, which still survives, to that effect, and a beautiful old house within the Cathedral close, now converted into a most interesting local museum, is called " Queen Berengaria's House." Unfortunately the legend is not borne out by the appearance of the house in question, as it is clearly a beautiful little building not older than the fourteenth century. The traditions attaching to her name, and the appearance of the cenotaph in the Cathedral, combine to give an idea that she was regarded as a benefactress to Le Mans in the thirty odd years of her widowhood. The modern French antiquaries describe her as La Reine Bérangère, dame douairière du Mans.

The monument consists of the ordinary recumbent effigy of thirteenth century style, but not of so fine a quality as the effigy of her husband at Rouen. It represents the queen in her robes of state : crowned with a heavy jewelled diadem confining a veil to her head, which may be the " widow's weed." In her hands she holds a small model of a building—presumably the Abbey of Epau—and from her waist girdle is suspended a hanging purse. Her feet rest on a small heraldic lion couchant. The stiff attitude of the arms and elbows is characteristic of thirteenth century work.

On the base of the queen's effigy are the words :—

Mausolœum istud serenissimœ Berengariœ
Anglorum Reginœ hujus Cœnobii Fundatricis
indita restauratum et in angustiorem locum
hunc translatum fuit in eoque recondita sunt

Ossa hœc quœ reperta fuerunt in antiquo tumulo
die 27 Maii Anno Domini 1672 Ex ecclesia Abbatiali
de pietate Dei translatum fuit et depositum in ecclesia cathedrali
die 2 Decembris 1821.

Richard Cœur de Lion died on 6th April, 1199, at the small fortress town of Chalus, between Limoges and Perigueux, belonging to his vassal Aymer, Vicomte de Limoges. Claiming, as suzerain, the whole of a treasure-trove found in the neighbourhood, he besieged the castle where it had been deposited, and whilst reconnoitring its defences, he was struck in the left shoulder by an arrow discharged from its walls.

The castle was soon taken, and its garrison of 38 men was hanged excepting the archer who had aimed the fatal arrow, Bertrand de Gourdon by name, who avowed when brought before the dying King, that revenge for his father's death at the King's hands, had prompted the act. Richard magnanimously spared the archer's life, but he is said to have been flayed alive after the King's death by the Brabançon soldiers.

The spot where Richard stood when he received his death-wound is still marked by a white stone called " Maumont."

Two monumental effigies were executed of Richard I. shortly after his death, and are still in existence at Fontevrault and in Rouen Cathedral respectively. Richard was buried in the Abbey of Fontevrault together with his father Henry II., and his mother Eleanor, and also the widow of his brother John, Isabella d' Angouléme. The four royal graves were decorated with life-size effigies which survive in a much mutilated condition, although the graves were destroyed in 1793. The effigy of Richard has been accounted a portrait, and from it the King has been pictured in many old history books, with their copper engravings, as a man with aquiline features and broad forehead, wearing a beard and moustache.

The effigy in the south choir aisle of Rouen Cathedral is equally authentic, but it represents the King as clean shaven ! He lies in the royal robes with a heavy jewelled crown on his head; in his left hand is the fleur-de-lisé sceptre whilst with his right he seems to pluck open the heavy cope. Around his waist is the jewelled baudrick, and at his feet lies a miniature lion couchant on a tuft of leafage in which several small animals, a rabbit, a lizard, etc., appear. The treatment of the sculpture is of the finest thirteenth century style, and this is apparent in spite of several extensive restorations of its surface, the replacing of the nose and chin, the fingers and various parts in the vestments.

The effigies of Fontevrault and Rouen are alike in their design, and also in their colossal size, as both measure $6\frac{1}{2}$ feet in height—this may not however have been the King's stature, many thirteenth century statues are of what was called the " heroic " scale.

Under the fine cenotaph figure at Rouen was buried the " lion-heart " of the great King. In 1867 this heart— a shrivelled morsel of human flesh enveloped in a piece of green taffety within a leaden case—was found in the place where it had lain for over seven centuries; it now reposes in the Rouen Museum. 'The cenotaph was removed by the Huguenots in 1563, and lost sight of until 1838. Since 1870 it has been restored to about the position it originally occupied on the south side of the high altar. The tomb-like base of elaborately panelled stonework is entirely modern, but the figure is undoubtedly original and very interesting; the following words are inscribed on the base:—

COR RICARDI REGIS ANGLORUM
COR LEONIS DICTI OBIIT ANNO
MCXCIX.

180 CYPRUS UNDER AN ENGLISH KING.

NOTE ON THE GENEALOGY OF RICHARD CŒUR DE LION THROUGH HIS MOTHER, ELEANOR DUCHESS OF ACQUITAINE.

William VII. Duke of Acquitaine, etc., and Philippa of Toulouse.

1127. William VIII. (b. 1099, d. 9.4.1137, the recluse of the Holy Sepulchre) and Aenor de Chateaulerault.
    1. Eleanor.
    2. Peronelle.
    3. William le Hardi.

1137. Eleanor (b. 1123, d. 1204) marr. Louis VII. of France, 22.7.1137.
    1. Marie, marr. Henry I. Count of Champagne.
    2. Alice, marr. Thibaut Count of Blois.

1152. Eleanor divorced, 18.3.1152, marr. Henry II. of England, 18.5.1152, (d. 1189).
    1. William (b. 1153, d. 1158.)
    2. Henry (b. 1154, affianced to Margaret, d. of Louis VII. 1158, marr. 1172, twice crowned King of England, d. 1182).
    3. Richard (b. 1157, aff. to Adela, d. of Louis VII., c. 1175, marr. Berengaria 1191).
    4. Maud (b. 1157, marr. Henry V. of Bavaria 1167, d. 1190).
    5. Geoffrey (b. 1158, marr. Constance of Brittany 1185, d. 1186).
    6. Eleanor (b. 1162, marr. Alphonso VIII. of Castile, 1177 d. ?)
    7. Joan (b. 1164, marr. William II. of Sicily 1176, d. 1195).
    8. John (b. 1166, marr. Isabella d. of Aymer Count of Angoulême d. 1216.)

1169. Duchy of Acquitaine ceded to Richard as Count of Poitou, for which he did homage to the French king (6.1.1171.)

INDEX.

Abelard, 118
Abruzzi, 23
Acquitaine, Duchy of, 180
Acre, 15, 32, 44, 54, 94, 120, 131, 132, 133, 137, 149, 150
—— Bishop of, 156
Acrotiri, temple, 100, 101
Adalia, 45
Adela, daughter of Louis VII., 180
Adolphus, Count of Holstein, 157
Adonis, 84
Aenor de Chateaulerault, 180
Agello, Matteo d', 33
Alain, Archdeacon of Lydda, 156, 160
Alaric, 31
Aleman Family, 157
Alexander III., Pope, 93
Alexis I., Byzantine Emperor, 62
Alice, Countess of Blois, 180
—— daughter of Baldwin II., 88
—— daughter of Isabella of Jerusalem, 95
—— (or Adela) daughter of Louis VII., 45, 47
Alphonso II., King of Arragon, 173
—— VIII., King of Castile, 180
Amadi (Hist.), 137, 138, 139, 140
Amalfi, 20, 25, 61
Amantea, 30, 31
Amathus, 54, 56, 65, 75
  described, 63, 64
  Feast at, 79–83
  Marriage of Berengaria at, 97–109
  Phœnician Colony, 64
Amaury I., 87. 89
—— II. v. Lusignan
Andronikos, Byzantine Emperor, 59, 62
Angelos, Isaac, Byzantine Emperor, 59, 60, 93
Angoulême, Pierre d', 150
Angulier Family, 142
Antioch, 21, 45, 46, 170
Apollo, 84
Apulia, 24, 25
Armenia, 21, 133, 170, 172, 176
Armenians capture Isaac Comnenus 59
Arms and accoutrement of twelfth century, 161, 164
Arsinœ, Bishopric, 119
Ascalon, 140

Astarte, or Ashtaroth, 64
Athlit, 133
Auch, Archbishop of, 74, 104, 166
Augustinian Abbeys, 133
Auley, Sir Fulk d', 80
Avignon, 9
Aymer, Count of Angoulême, 180
—— Vicomte de Limoges, 177
Bagnara Monastery, 35
Baldwin, Archbishop of Canterbury, 103, 168
—— de Bethshan, 161
—— Count of Flanders, 131, 176
—— I. King of Jerusalem, 88
—— II. ,, 88, 89
—— III. ,, 89
—— IV. ,, 89
—— V. ,, 89
Basil, Byzantine Emperor, 62
Bayonne, Bishop of, 74, 105, 166
Beauvais, Bishop of, 120, 121, 144, 146
" Beffroi," used by Richard I., 39
Benedict of Peterboro, (Hist.), 51, 87, 101, 169, 170
Benedictines, Abbeys of, 30, 133
Benevento, 61
Berengaria—
  Arrival at Amathus, 57, 58, 69
  Cenotaph of, 176, 177
  Coronation of, 102, 172, 176
  Escort of, 44, 45
  Marriage of, 97-109
  Return to Europe of, 173
Bernard, St. (of Clairvaux,) 1, 14, 134
Bethlehem, Bishop of, 155
Blanchegarde Family, 110, 157
—— Fortress, 87
Bohemond II., Prince of Antioch, 88
Bonifazio Straits, 17
Bouchart, Arnaut, Sir, 138, 139, 140
Bouillon, Godfrey de, 1, 61, 88, 121
Brannus, Usurper, 93
Bras de Fer, William, 26, 60, 61
Bries, De, Family, 157
Brindisi, Archbishop of, 155
Brittany, Princess of. 173
Bruno, St., 33
Buono, Architect, 24
Burgundy, Duke of, 166
Busento, Tomb of Alaric at, 31
Butler Family, 80

INDEX.

Byzantine Empire, 59, 60-62, 63
Cæsar, Julius, 32
Cagne, William de, 144
Calabria, Richard in, 24, 25, 30, 50
Cantara Castle, 124, 125
Capraja island, 22, 23
Caprano, Castle of, 24
Capri island, 23, 24
Carmelites, Abbeys of, 133
Carnot, Bishop of, 166
Castel dell'Ovo, 24
Cava Monastery, 25
Cefalu, Richard & Tancred at, 41-43
Celestine III., Pope, 156
Cephalonia, 26
Cesnola, 64
Cetraro, Benedictines at, 30
Chaluz, Richard dies at, 163
Charlemagne, 84
Chatillon, Reginald de, 63, 91, 92
Chinon Castle, 173, 174
Chirokitia, Isaac Comnenus at, 75, 77
Chittim v. Kitium
Choniates Niketas, 59, 62
Circe island, 23
Cistercians, 134
Clement XI., Pope, 172
Clifford, Rosamund, 45, 161
Cnidus ruins, 54
Coggeshale, (Hist.), 169
Colossi Castle, 137
Comnena, Anna, 163.
——Maria, 89, 93.
——Theodora, 89.
Comnenus, Isaac, 54, 56, 58, 62, 63, 68, 71, 110, 120–125, 127, 174
Conrad, Bishop of Hildersheim, 155, 157
Constance of Brittany, 171
——Wife of Henry VI. of Germany, 33, 176
Constantia, Archbishop of, 115, 119
   Arrival of Crusaders, 32, 116
   Cathedral, 71
   Description of, 111, 112
   Richard's departure from, 129
Constantine I. of Armenia, 170
——VII., Emperor, 62, 119
Constantinople, 3, 43, 62, 114
Conway, Martin, Sir, 19
Corfu, 126
Corsairs, 23
Corsica, 18
Courcy, Robert de, 118, 119
Courtenay, Agnes de, 89
——Jocelin de, 91
Crecy, Longbow used at, 20, 162, 163
Crete, Fleet at, 52

Crusaders at Acre, 120, 131
   Armour of, 161-164
   Capture of Amathus by, 63, 65–75
   at Rhodes, 53
Crusades, 60-62
Cyprus, Richard's occupation of 56, 121-130, 132
   Templars in, 133
   Wine of, 21
Dampierre family, 142 157
Darum Fortress, 148, 149
Diano valley, 29-30
Diyeni or Dioscure, 84, 85
Djebail, capture of, 21
Doria family, 19, 21-22
Drogo de Merle, 120
Dubois, William, 57
Du Cange (Hist.), 59
Dugdale (Hist.), 79
Ed-darum v. Darum.
Edessa, 170
Edmondsbury Abbey, 78-79
Edward I. of England, 162
El Arish, 148
Elba island, 22, 23
Eleanor, Queen of France and England—
   Berengaria's marriage arranged by, 47, 48
   Buried at Fontevrault, 178
   Genealogy of, 180
   at Jerusalem, 45, 46, 89
   at Reggio, 44
   Travels of, 173
——wife of Alphonso VIII. of Castile, 180
Encomi, 122
Epau Abbey, 176
Eremberga, 32
Ernoul (Hist.), 90
Etna, 31
Eufemia, S., Abbey, 32, 33
Eustace, Count of Lorrain, 88
Evreux, Bishop, 74, 103, 104
Faro, the, 35
Fatina, v. Cefalu.
Fieschi family, 1-9, 21, 22
Fontevrault Abbey, 178
Frederick I. Barbarossa, 2, 3
——II. Emperor of Germany, 174, 177
Fulk of Anjou, 88, 89, 172
Gaetan Republic, 23, 25
Gaillard, Chateau, 24
Galleys, description of, 15, 16
Gaza, 148, 149
Gelnhausen Palace, 155
Genoa, Richard's reception at, 19-21

INDEX. 183

Geoffrey, Archbishop of York, 172
——Master, (Hist.), 43, 117, 119
    121, 141, 144, 150
Gibbon (Hist.), 31.
Giblet, Renier de, 155
——v. Djebail.
Gioja, town, 34
Glanville, Ralph de, 168
Godfrey de Bouillon, 1, 61, 88, 121
Gorgona island, 22
Gourdon, Bertrand de, 177
Greek culture, 64
——Plot to murder Templars, 139, 140
Green, (Hist.) 33
Gregory VIII., Pope, 2
Grey, Sir Henry de, 80
Griffons, 29, 58, 165, 166, 167
Grimaldi family, 19, 21, 22
——Frederick, 20
——Grimaldo, 20
——Obert, 20
Guiscard Drogo, 26, 27
——Humphrey, 26, 27
——Robert, 26, 32, 60, 61
Gunther, Bishop of Bamberg, 78, 79
Hackett, Dr., 59, 94, 119, 126, 156
Hakluyt, Richard, 164
Halicarnassus Mausoleum, 53, 54
Hampton, Sir David, 80
Hashish or Assassins, 144-146
Harcourt, Roger de, 57, 75
Hattim, Mt., 92
Hautville family, 26, 27
Hayton, Armenian King, 171
Helena, Emp., 101
Henfrid de Toron, 86, 96
Henry II. of England, 2, 161 170, 171, 178, 180
——III. of England, 135
——V. of Bavaria, 180
——VI. of Germany, 154, 156, 174, 176
——Count of Champagne, 132, 144, 145, 146-148, 151, 153, 154, 180
Heraclius, Patriarch 91
Hereford, Prior of, 142, 143
Hildersheim, Bishop of, 155, 158-160
Hodierna dau. of Baldwin II., 88
Holy Roman Empire, 156
——Sepulchre, 89
Honorius II., Pope, 133
Hoveden, Roger de, 17, 33, 169
Ibelin family, 153, 154
——Fortress, 87
Innocent III. Pope, 175, 178

Isabella of Angoulême, 178
——Dau. of Leo III. of Armenia,171
——Wife of Conrad de Monferrat, 89, 93, 95, 132, 137, 145, 146-148
Ischia island, 23
Ismail 6th Iman, 145
Jaffa, 70, 73, 114
Jerusalem, Capture of, 2
    Crown, 132
    Coats of arms, 1
    Eleanor's arrival at, 45, 46
    Feudal Kingdom, 88-94
Joan, Queen of Sicily, 33, 39, 80, 101, 173, 180
John, King of England, 99. 142-145, 169, 176, 180
——Saint, shrine of, 71, 72
Kalopsyda, 123
Karpasion Bishopric, 119
Kerma Bishopric, 119
Kilani, 111
Kingsford, C. L., 137
Kitium, 113, 114, 119
Knowles, Sir Thomas, 80
Kophino, 113
Kouklia, 123
Kurion Bishopric, 119
Kyrenia, 119, 127
Kythrea Bishopric, 119, 126
Lambert family, 142
Lapethos Bishopric, 119
Laodicea, Archdeacon of, 156, 157
    Battle of, 45
Larnaca, 24, 30
Lazarus, Tomb of, 113, 114
Ledra, or Lefkosia v. Nicosia.
Leicester, Earl of, 80, 105
Le Mans Cathedral, 176, 177
Lembriac, Hugh de, 21
Leo II. of Armenia, 170, 171
——VI. of Armenia, 171
Levant privileges granted to Merchants, 21
Lombards, 36, 61
Longchamp, William de, 142, 161, 168, 169, 172
Louis VII., 1, 4, 45, 89, 158, 180
——XVIII. Court etiquette of, 11
Lucan, Poet, 22
Lusignan, de—
——Amaury, 87, 153, 155-160, 161, 171, 175, 176
——Geoffrey, 86, 87, 153, 154
——Guy, 86, 87, 90, 91, 92, 94, 95, 111, 113, 132, 137, 138, 151-153, 158, 170, 174, 175
——Hugh I. Count of Poitou, 87
——Hugh II., 87

# INDEX.

Lusignan, de—
——Hugh VIII., 87
——Hugh IX., 87
——James I., 171
Lyons, encampment at, 3, 5-13
Lytton, Sir Gilbert de, 80
Magan, Lieut., 64
Magna Græcia, 61
Manuel, Byzantine Emperor, 70, 93
Margaret, dau. of Louis VII., 180
Margaritone, Admiral, 60
Margat Fortress, 128, 174
Marie Countess of Champagne, 180
——Countess of Toulouse, 128, 173-176
Marseilles, 3, 13-17
Mary, niece of Sibylla, 95
Mas Latrie, 44, 45, 56, 67, 103, 136, 137, 140, 141, 148, 150, 151, 152, 153 169, 170, 172, 176
"Mategriffon," 42
Matthew of Paris, 135
Maud, Wife of Henry V. of Bavaria, 180
Mechitaristi monks, 172
Melfi, City, 24-27
Messina taken by Richard, 32, 36-39, 47, 49, 68, 165-169
Mileto, 31-34
Milicent, dau. of Baldwin II., 88
Millar, Walter, Archbishop of Palermo, 33
Mimars family, 157, 131
Mirabel Fortress, 87
Montferrat, Boniface de, King of Thessaly, 92, 93
——Conrad de, 87, 92, 93, 94, 97, 132, 137, 141, 142, 144-146
——Renier de, 92, 93
——William de, 89, 92, 93
Monreale, Archbishop of, 166
Monte Cassino, 30
Monte Christo island, 22
Montereau, Pierre de, 118, 119
Monticchio, Lake, 28
Morgan, J. de (Hist.), 172
Moustri family, 142
Muro castle, 25
Naples, Richard at, 24, 25, 61
Nazareth, Archbishop of, 156
Nefin family, 131, 157
Nemevos Bishopric, 119
Neophytos, Hermit, 59, 62
Nesle Jean de, Gov. of Bruges, 175
Nevers, Count of, 166
Neville, Tombstone of, 80, 81, 131
Nicholas, Royal Chaplain, 101, 102

Nicosia, Amaury crowned in, 156-60
Royal Palace in, 160
Templars at. 136, 139-142
Nores, de, family, 80-81, 131, 157
Normandy, 1, 27
Norreys v. Nores
Observant Friars, 164
Ormonde, Earl of, 80, 105, 109
Palermo, 40, 62
Palmarola island, 23
Papho Bishopric, 119
Payen, Hugh de, 112, 133
Pediæs River, 115, 123, 126
Perch, Count of, 166
Peronelle, daughter of William VIII., 180
Peter the Hermit, 1, 61
Philip Augustus of France, 6, 40, 42, 43, 44, 89, 146-148, 166
——Prince of Antioch, 171
Philippa of Toulouse, 180
Phœnicians, 64
Pietra Santa Church, 25
Pisa, Archbishop of, 166
——Berengaria at, 44
Pisano Nicolo, 118, 119
Pisans, Corsairs, 23
Poitiers, Cross-bow used at, 20, 162, 163
Ponza island, 23
Porto Venere Fortress, 22
Potenza, 29.
Provost family, 131
Ptolemies, 101
Ralph the Chamberlain, 128
Ratisbon, German Army at, 3
Raymond, Count of Tripoli, 86, 88, 90-92
——St. Giles, Count of Toulouse, 173, 174, 175, 176
Raynauld de Chatillon, 63
Reggio, Berengaria at, 29, 44, 47, 48
Renand (Hist.), 96
Rethel, Count of, 88
Rhodes, Richard at, 53, 54, 56
Rhone Bridge, 7
Rhupen, 59, 170
Richard I.—
at Amathus, 65, 85
at Acre, 128, 321
at Ascalon, 140
at Cefalu, 41, 43
Court, etiquette of, 11, 13
Death of, 151, 174, 717
Effigy of, 176, 177, 178
Genealogy, 180
at Genoa, 18, 22
Incident of hawk, 34, 35
King-malrer, 140

INDEX. 185

Richard I.—
  Levies raised by, 2-3
  Lyons, at, 5-13
  Marriage of, 97-109
  News of John's conduct, 142, 149
  Prisoner in Germany, 154, 171
  Pursuit of Isaac Comnenus, 75
  Siege of Messina, 165-168
  Travels, 18-55
  ——of Devizes, 33, 47, 51, 68, 103, 128, 165, 172
Robert, Earl of Leicester, 75
Rochemaure Castle, 9
Roger, King of Naples, 25, 32
Rose of Acquitaine, v. Eleanor.
Rouen, Archbishop of, 166, 168
——Effigy of Richard I. at, 177, 178
Sablé, Robert de, 136
Saint—
——George, 21, 105
——John, Order of, 71, 73, 111
——Lucido, Monastery, 30
——Mark's, Venice, 43
——Nicholas Fortress, 17
——Paul's Chapter, 74
——Simeon, port of, 21
——Spyridon Church, 126
——Thomas of Canterbury, 74
——Victor, Abbey, 14
Saladin, 68, 89-92, 152, 166
Salamis v. Constantia.
Saleph in Cilicia, 3
Salerno, 24, 25
Sancho VI. King of Navarre, 44, 101, 176
Saracens, 2, 61, 152, 153, 162
Sardinia, 18
Scalea, 24.
Schlumberger (Writer), 176
Scott, Sir Walter, 152
Scylla, 31
Sephardin, Saladin's brother, 152
Servia, Queen Eleanor in, 44
Sibylla, wife of Guy de Lusignan, 89, 91, 92, 93-95, 132, 172
——wife of Roger, King of Naples, 25
Sicily, Richard's visit to, 36 44
Soli, Bishopric, 119
Spartavento Cape, 44, 51
Spezia, 22
Spinola family, 19, 21, 22
Stromboli 31, 32
Stuteville, Lord of, 75
Tabarie family, 131, 142
Taillebourg, Bourgoyne de, 87
Tamassos Bishopric, 119
Tancred, King, 24, 39, 41, 166, 167

Taurus mountains, 127
Templars, order of,
  purchase Cyprus, 137
  History, 133-139
  Plot to murder, 139, 140
  Richard's arrangement about Cyprus with, 111, 150
Thenouri family, 142
Theodora, sister of I. Angelos, 59, 93
I. Comnenus ransomed by, 59
Thibaut Count of Blois, 180
Tiberias, Battle of, 2
Tortosa Fortress, 33
Toulouse, Countess of, 128, 173-176
Tours, 3
Trani, Archbishop of, 155
Transinges, Odo de, 144
Tremethousha v. Tremythus.
Tremythus, 119, 124, 125, 127
Tripoli, 131, 150, 151
Troyes, Council of, 131
Turcopoliers, 134
Turnham, Robert de, 50, 128, 132, 134, 138
——Stephen de, 50, 56, 57, 65, 128, 150, 173
Tyre, 131, 141, 142, 146, 147, 148
Tyrhennian Sea, 23
Uniats, 171, 172
Urban III. Pope, 2
Val di Diano, 29
Venice, Doges Palace, 20, 112
Venosa Abbey, 26, 27
Venus, 22, 63, 64, 84, 85
Vezelay Abbey, 3, 4
Vinsauf Geoffrey de (Hist.) 7, 8, 11, 18, 33, 38, 41, 43, 44, 56, 67, 68, 79, 120 165,, 169 170
Viollet le Duc, 28, 43, 109, 146, 158
Visconti family, 131
Vultura, monte, 25, 28
Westminster, First Parliament at, 20
William I. King of Sicily, 26, 60
——II. King of Sicily, 33, 59 166, 178, 186
——III. de Montferrat, 92, 93
——VIII. Count of Poitou, 46, 180
——Archbishop of Tyre, 2, 67, 90, 136, 147, 150, 151, 155
——Le Hardi King of France, 180
——Long Epee, Montferrat, 92
——of Newbury, 169
——Son of Eleanor of Acquitaine. 180
Wine. 81
York, Archibishop of, 103
Zampognari, 42

OTHER ZENO PUBLICATIONS

FINLAY, GEORGE
HISTORY OF THE GREEK REVOLUTION AND THE REIGN OF KING OTHO.
A Reprint with revised index and select bibliography and foreword by Prof. Douglas Dakin, of vols. vi and vii of George Finlay, *A History of Greece from its Conquest by the Romans to the Present time* 164 B.C.– A.D. 1864. Edited by Rev. H. F. Tozer, Oxford, 1877: London 1971.
ISBN 0 900834 12 9   2 vols. in one   £10·50 p.

FINLAY, GEORGE
DESPATCHES TO THE TIMES DURING THE YEARS 1864–1875 AND OTHER DOCUMENTS.
"*Finlay's despatches to* The Times *from 1864 prove a valuable source for the early years of the reign of King George I. They form as it were an additional volume to his history.*"—Prof. D. Dakin.
Edited by Prof. Douglas Dakin.   Spring 1974.   About £4·50 p.
ISBN 0 900834 24 2

MARITI, GIO.
TRAVELS IN THE ISLAND OF CYPRUS.
Translated from the Italian by C. D. Cobham, with contemporary accounts of the sieges of Nicosia and Famagusta
By Gio P. Contarini and Count Nestor Martinengo.
Demy 8vo., vii+199 pp., London, 1909; Reprinted 1971   £3
ISBN 0 900834 20 X   LCCC 77–180477

ORR, CAPT. C. W. J.
CYPRUS UNDER BRITISH RULE.
Demy 8vo., 192 pp., folded map, London, 1918; Reprinted 1972 £3
ISBN 0 900834 19 6.   LCCC 70–180478

KOUMOULIDES, JOHN T. A.
CYPRUS AND THE WAR OF GREEK INDEPENDENCE 1821–1829.
With foreword by Douglas Dakin, with 2 ills. and map, 2nd edition revised and enlarged. London: Zeno 1974
ISBN 0 900834 81 1   £3·50 p.
ISBN 0 900834 82 X paper covers   £2

ALASTOS, DOROS
CYPRUS IN HISTORY, a Survey of 5,000 years
2nd edition in Preparation.

JEFFERY, GEORGE
A DESCRIPTION OF THE HISTORIC MONUMENTS OF CYPRUS.
Studies in the Archaeology and Architecture of the Island, with illustrations from measured drawings and photographs.
First published 1918. Reprint in Preparation   About £4·50 p.
ISBN 0 900834 84 6

KIRKWALL, VISCOUNT (*Editor*)
FOUR YEARS IN THE IONIAN ISLANDS. Their political and social conditions. With a History of the British Protectorate. In 2 vols.
First published London 1864. Reprint in Preparation About £8·50 p.
ISBN 0 900834 23 4.   LCCC 73–184834

PRINTED BY OFFSET LITHOGRAPHY BY
BILLING & SONS LIMITED, GUILDFORD AND LONDON